CW01494904

A Brief Introduction to Egyptian Coins *and* Currency

Peter Watson

authorHOUSE®

AuthorHouse™ UK
1663 Liberty Drive
Bloomington, IN 47403 USA
www.authorhouse.co.uk
Phone: 0800.197.4150

Published by AuthorHouse   10/15/2014

ISBN: 978-1-4969-9019-8 (sc)
ISBN: 978-1-4969-9018-1 (hc)
ISBN: 978-1-4969-9020-4 (e)

Contents

Preface

There are many books which consider the coins and currency of particular periods of the history of Egypt, some of which are noted in the bibliographies, but there are none which cover the whole of that history. This book aims to amend that by providing an introductory overview of Egyptian coins from their earliest days in the late Pharaonic period to modern times.

In addition to this main aim of providing a chronological account of the Egyptian coinage, a secondary aim is to relate the coins of the different periods to the daily lives of the people living at those times. However while there is thus a historic theme, the book is about coins. The historic comments are only to provide settings for these coins and they certainly do not provide a complete account of the history of Egypt. For example while there were over sixty Roman emperors up to the division of the Roman Empire in 395 A.D., only a few are noted in this work. Similar comments could be made about the Abbasid caliphs, or the Mamluk and Ottoman sultans.

From each of these series of rulers, coins have been selected from those rulers who

a/ introduced some change into the coinage, especially if the newly introduced coin-type persisted well beyond the reign of the ruler, or

b/ had a long reign, and/or produced a large volume of coins, or

c/ were famous, or d/ left notable buildings in Egypt, which are mentioned in the text.

There is of course a degree of subjectivity in the selection in each of these groups.

Egypt nowadays is an independent country with well defined borders. In the past however this was not always so. There are two different situations worth noting. When Egypt was independent, its borders would ebb and flow: sometimes it was larger than now and sometimes smaller. For example some Ptolemaic kings ruled over parts of Libya, the Levant and even Cyprus. On the other hand, sometimes Egypt was not independent but part of a larger state and was ruled from outside what is currently Egypt. Both of these situations have consequences for the currency

In the first scenario, Egyptian coins could circulate and even be minted in other (current day) countries and would be seen as coins of those countries, and nowadays those countries might, for example, see Egyptian ptolemaic coins as part of their numismatic history. In the second situation, coins from the dominant external state would be used and even minted in Egypt, perhaps with an egyptian mint mark. For the purpose of this work such coins, minted in Egypt with an appropriate mintmark, are treated as Egyptian.

As this book covers many different currencies, a list of coin denominations is provided at the end of this preface, along with a short glossary of numismatic terms.

There are coin and currency illustrations occurring towards the end of the book after the text. In the text, a number in brackets and in bold print refers to an item in these illustrations. Concerning these illustrations, there is a list, the 'Key to the currency illustrations', giving details of all the coins. While most illustrations show only one side of a coin, this list in many cases includes details of the designs on both sides of the coin. It also includes the legends which on some coins are very worn and difficult to read. It also gives details such as coin sizes, weights, the metals of which they are made, and their dates. Thus this list includes a considerable amount of numismatic information not included in the general text.

In addition, the list in the left hand column, includes dates, which along with information in the list, provide a numismatic "Timeline".

From this it is noted incidentally that in some centuries many coins were produced in Egypt, but in a couple, i.e. the fifth and eighth, relatively few coins were minted there.

In the text at some points a name may occur in brackets, e.g. (Tacitus). This indicates a book in the Bbliography from which the point is taken and may be followed up.

As Egypt has been ruled by many different peoples, it has used many languages. Its currency has exhibited five different languages: ancient Egyptian, Greek, Latin, Arabic and English. A brief note on transliteration might be worthwhile here, as the reader might come across a name in this book spelt differently in another book. The written forms of two of the languages do not include the range of vowels used in English. Thus given the hieroglyphics of a famous queen English writers usually put Nefertiti, as in this text, see item (133), while German and other authors put Nofretete (Zauzich 1992). Similarly the conqueror of Istanbul is usually named in English as Mohammed, while in Turkish accounts he is usually named Mehmed. When names in Arabic script are spelt in roman letters, the same sound might be symbolised by different letters by different writers. For example a famous Mamluk sultan is sometimes named as Kaitbay, as in this text, and is sometimes written as Qa'it bay. Similarly the name of an early group of caliphs, the Umayyads, is sometimes written in different ways such as the Ommayyads or the Ummmayyids.

The illustrations of the coins and banknotes by Sam Watson provide one of the most valuable aspects of the work. I am grateful to him for them and to him, to Alan Humphries and Richard Bourne for their helpful commentaries on drafts of this work and I would also like to thank Sam and Anne Watson for comments on the script.

Coins, currency, weights and related items

In the following 'pl' stands for 'plural'.

Ae (x)	We do not know what the names were for many bronze coins of the Greek and Roman periods. So such a coin is often referred to as Ae (x). There are 2 usages of this in the numismatic literature. In some books, in Ae(x) the x stands for the precise diameter of the coin in millimetres. In other books the x will be 1, 2, 3 or 4, and Ae(x) indicates that the coin belongs to one of several different size groups, with 1 referring to the group with the largest coins. In most cases in this work the first of these procedures will be used
Akce,	The first coin of the Ottoman Empire, silver about 1.2g.
Antoninianus,	Roman silver coin, introduced by Caracalla, equal in weight to 1 ½ denarii, perhaps tariffed at 2 denarii
Argenteus	Silver coin of Diocletian's reforms, roughly the same in size and weight as the old denarius
Ashrafi,	A Mamluk gold coin
Athens,owl,	A tetradrachm depicting an owl

Aureus,	Roman coin (1/60 lb of gold), originally worth 25 denarii
Centenionalis	Bronze coin introduced by Constantius II
Chalkon	Small Greek coin, in the Ptolemaic period worth 1/8 Obol.
Deben	Ancient Egyptian weight, approx 91 grams
Denarius,	The basic original Roman silver coin, (pl denarii)
Drachm	Basic coin of Greece, and also Egypt under the Ptolemies
Dinar,	Arabic gold coin
Dirhem,	Standard silver coin of Arabic currencies
Fals,	Early Islamic copper coin (pl. fulus)
Follis,	Roman bronze coin introduced in Diocletian's reforms, initially with slight silver content or wash, (pl folles)
Guersh	Egyptian silver coin, sometimes called a piastre
Kurus,	Turkish (Ottoman) coin
Lira	Gold Ottoman coin in the reformed coinage of 1844
Mangir	Ottoman copper coin
Miliaresion	Byzantine silver coin
Millieme	Egyptian coin worth 1/10 Piastre
Mina	Ancient weight, approximately equal to, and often translated as, a pound
Nummus	Basic bronze late Roman and Byzantine coin, (pl nummi, sometimes nummia)
Obol,	Small Greek coin, initially silver, worth 1/6 drachm. There are also related coins e.g. diobol, hemiobol etc.
Para	Egyptian &/or Turkish coin, originally silver, later copper
Piastre	Widespread coin denomination, e.g. of Egypt & Turkey
Pound	Egyptian coin, originally gold worth 100 guersh
Sestertius	A basic Roman orichalcum coin, worth ¼ denarius
Shekel	Originally a near-east weight, later also a coin
Solidus,	Roman gold coin introduced by Constantine, 1/72 of a pound of gold, i.e. lighter than the Aureus
Siliqua	Roman silver coin introduced by Constantine, later reduced to 2.25 gr. silver
Sultani	Initial gold coin of the Ottoman Empire.
Talent	Ancient weight equal to 60 Mina

Tetradrachm	Standard medium to large sized silver coin of ancient Greece
Zeri Mahbub	Ottoman gold coin
Zolota	Ottoman silver coin, worth ¾ Kurus
Bank Notes,	
LE.'x'	This, in relation to an Egyptian banknote, indicates the note is valued at 'x' Egyptian pounds.

Numismatic glossary

Ae(x)	Coin denomination, see the list above.
A.H.	A dating system, Anno Hegirae, see Appendix.
Billon	A mixture of silver and another metal, with the silver being less than 50%.
Currency	Anything that flows from hand to hand:- coins, banknotes or any medium of exchange which is accepted.
Debasement	This is when a government decreases the amount of a precious metal in a coin, but still issues the coin at its original face value.
Denomination	The name given to a class of coins, in which the coins have a specific value.
Exergue	Small space below the main design on a coin, sometimes separated from it by a line.
Fineness	The degree of precious metal in an alloy. For example, 90% fine means 90% of the precious metal mixed with 10% of a cheaper metal.
Kalima	The basic Moslem statement of faith.
Legend	The inscription on a coin.
Mint mark	A symbol or mark on a coin, indicating where it was produced.
Obverse	The side of a coin which bears the ruler's portrait or name, or the most important legend, often called 'heads'.
Regnal date	This numeral designates the number of years of a sovereign's reign that have elapsed, calculated from the date of accession.

Reverse	The opposite side of a coin to the obverse, sometimes called 'tails'
Tokens,	Unofficially issued coins, used instead of official coins, often when there is a shortage of the latter.
Tughra	The signature of an Ottoman or other Sultan, often stylised.
Type	A group of coins with a design distinguishing them from other coins.

Ancient Egypt

<u>Money and weights in ancient civilisations.</u>

In the advanced civilisation of ancient Egypt, long before coins were invented, people exchanged goods. In this barter economy to help them in their transactions they needed something, some commodity, to act as a standard of value and means of calculating what was worth what. Their transactions could get quite complex as is seen in the Rhind papyrus of the sixteenth century B.C. (Robins & Shute 1967), which is perhaps the oldest mathematics textbook in the world. In that, as an example, it is suggested that in order to exchange loaves for beer (both of which vary in quality) one has to relate them both to the amount of grain needed to produce them.

It may be useful to recall that the idea of "money" existed before that of "coins".

In early times, when there was a barter economy, money was any commodity which facilitated the exchange of goods. Many types of commodity were so used: grain as in the above example, cattle, pieces of iron or of a precious metal etc. In order to enable this process to take place people needed to be able to specify the weights, especially of the commodity being used as money. Such weights of commodities eventually themselves came to be used to specify the value of items. In the Bible the patriarch, Abraham, to obtain a grave site for his wife, "weighed 400 shekels of silver which was the current money, for the merchant" (Genesis 23). That is, he used a weight of bullion silver as money long before coins existed, a shekel being at that time a unit of weight not a coin. Similarly, later Solomon constructing his buildings in Jerusalem, adorned them with shields each containing three mina of gold (I Kings 10), a mina being approximately one pound weight, with one mina equal to sixty shekels. Shortly afterwards the Pharaoh Sheshonk invaded Palestine and took away these gold shields (2 Chronicles 12) and other booty.

Somewhat later, the Pharoah Necho II, to reassert his control over the region, extracted a tribute of 100 talents of silver and a talent of gold from the Israelites (2 Kings 23), a talent being a weight equal to sixty minas.

The above weights, which were used throughout the region, were probably of Babylonian origin, like the five mina weight illustrated here.

A Babylonian five mina weight

In addition to these, in early Egypt there was a local unit of weight, the deben (approximately 91 grams), divided into ten 'kites'. There is an example of the use of this in the twelfth century Harris papyrus (Budge 1926, Gardiner 1961), which is the most magnificent of all the ancient Egyptian state archives in the possession of the British Museum. In that we learn that Rameses III donated 18252 debens of gold and silver, in addition to vast quantities of food, to the temple at Thebes. Also, turning from the lives of Pharaohs to those of citizens, in another twelfth century papyrus (Gardiner 1961), we read the tale of an Egyptian, Wenamun, going to Palestine by ship, who is robbed on board of his money. After remonstrating at his destination with the local prince, he eventually is able to retrieve, the papyrus tells us, '30 debens of silver'. The deben slowly changed and finally five equalled one mina.

So early Egyptians like other people of the region facilitated transactions by using money in the form of weights of commodities, particularly precious metals, long before coins were used.

Weighing gold, from the tomb of Rekhmire at Thebes

It is perhaps worth noting that one of the weights in the tomb illustration is similar to the Babylonian weight of five mina illustrated earlier.

The deben was originally a weight but eventually became, much later after the development of coins, a measure of value with one deben of silver equal to five silver staters (tetradrachms).

Early Egyptian writing was in hieroglyphics. These were often monumental, chiselled into walls etc. and too clumsy for everyday use and so evolved into a cursive script: hieratic, which was used in daily accounts etc. In about 700 BC this evolved into an even more cursive script: demotic, which is seen on the Rosetta stella.

Early coins

Eventually, to avoid the need for repeated weighings, standardised weights of metal, marked by the issuing authority were introduced. These were the first coins, initially produced in what is now Turkey but then rapidly spread to places around the Aegean sea. Of these currencies one of the first to attain a mass circulation was that of Athens. The main coin of this currency was the tetradrachm, a medium sized silver coin, which had on one side an owl, - these coins are often called the 'owls' of Athens-, by the side of the owl are Greek letters standing for Athens, to show where the coin was minted. Some of these eventually circulated in countries around the Eastern Mediterranean and some imitations of them were minted in some of these countries. In Egypt some of these imitations **(1)** were struck in the fifth century, most likely to pay for Greek mercenaries (von Reden, 2010). Egypt at the time was a province of the Persian Empire, so some of these imitations (1) had an Egyptian demotic (or Persian) inscription instead of the Greek letters.

Shortly after Egypt had been freed from Persian rule, one of the pharaohs, Nectanebo II (360 – 342 B. C.), issued a very rare gold coin

(2), with a hieroglyphic inscription, as illustrated in the Appendix. Why he produced just this one type of coin isn't known.

Later Alexander III of Macedonia, (Alexander the Great), defeated the Persians, who had again taken over Egypt, and he acquired Egypt along with the rest of the Persian Empire. After his victory over the Persians he travelled around his empire to consolidate his hold. When in Egypt he founded the city of Alexandria. Being from Macedonia where people were accustomed to having coins, on his travels he produced coins in many places to pay his troops and at each place the coins would be stamped with a mark to indicate where they had been minted. He had silver tetradrachms **(3)** and small bronze coins minted in Egypt at Memphis, the tetradrachms bear the Memphis mint mark; the Khnum (a rams head and an Isis crown as illustrated on the left hand side of the coin).

THE PTOLEMAIC KINGDOM

Some Ptolemaic monarchs and their coins

After the death of Alexander the Great (323 B.C.), his generals shared out his empire. The general Ptolemy acquired Egypt and surrounding territories. Initially he ruled as Satrap (i.e. Governor) but later declared himself King of Egypt. Externally and along the borders of his territories he was involved in a lot of wars and skirmishes with other generals about who should possess which pieces of land.

Within Egypt he founded the city of Ptolemais, now called el Manshah. In Alexandria he made improvements and initiated the idea of a library and 'museum', which was to be a kind of college where researchers: scientists, philosophers and writers, could stay and study. He himself wrote a biography of Alexander. Though the original is lost, we know of it as the roman writer Arrian based his "Life of Alexander" on it. Ptolemy introduced the Serapis cult, which involved a fusion of two of the main Egyptian deities, i.e. Osiris and Apis, establishing it initially at Memphis.

Before the Ptolemaic dynasty there had been occasional coins circulating and even being minted in Egypt but Ptolemy I established the first effective mass coinage there. When he was Satrap, his initial silver coin was similar to those of Alexander the Great, with a portrait of Alexander as obverse and a seated Zeus on the reverse. This was shortly followed by tetradrachms (4) again depicting Alexander but with Athena as a warrior on the reverse. This was the guardian goddess of Pella the capital of Macedonia and recalls the Macedonian origin of the regime. These coins also exhibited the personal badge of Ptolemy, an eagle standing on a thunderbolt.

When he became king he issued gold (5), silver and bronze coins. Some of his silver tetradrachms (6) had his portrait as obverse and an eagle on the reverse and his bronze coins, depicted Zeus as on (7) and an eagle (9). On these coins, on the reverse, there is the legend

ΠΤΟΛΕΜΑΙΟΥ ΒΑΣΙΛΕΩΣ, King Ptolemy. These two coins types provided the standard designs and legend which recurred throughout the Ptolemaic coinage. Initially the first of his silver tetradrachms were the same standard as the coins of Athens, i.e. about seventeen grams, but later he reduced them to about fourteen grams because of limited silver resources. This was one of the factors leading eventually to Egypt becoming a closed currency zone where only Ptolemaic coins circulated. Similarly the bronze coins were reduced in size and weight. There is some controversy, (von Reden 2007), as to the value of the bronze coins, for example was the large one, Ae 42, illustrated **(9)** a three obol or a drachm. Ptolemy moved the mint from Memphis to Alexandria, which became the main Ptolemaic mint.

Ptolemy II, the son of Ptolemy I, developed the country financially, by improving Egypt's agriculture and reopening the disused canal between the Nile and the Red sea.

The Pharos lighthouse in Alexandria, commissioned by his father, was completed early in his reign. This will be seen on coins mentioned below. He developed the Library and Museum in Alexandria along the lines proposed by his father making the city a leading centre for the sciences and arts. After the death of his wife Arsinoe II he renamed the Fayoum as the Arsinoite nome in her honour.

On some of his coins, including tetradrachms, Ptolemy II portrayed not himself but Ptolemy I **(8)**. This set a precedent; tetradrachms and other coins of the future rulers of the dynasty depicted Ptolemy I, with variations in style, not the ruler issuing the coin, though fortunately some other coins of these rulers did include their portraits. Eventually there were fifteen rulers called Ptolemy.

Ptolemy II introduced a range of sizes to the bronze coins including some quite large ones, for example initially one weighing about a deben, although this was soon reduced. These large coins were continued by his son Ptolemy III **(9)** and others. After the death of his wife Arsinoe II, Ptolemy II issued a gold coin to commemorate her. This is discussed below and is seen on a modern stamp. In addition he issued other gold coins, which also are noted below.

Ptolemy III, continuing the activity of his grandfather and father, restored some Pharaonic temples and he started the building of a new temple at Edfu. This temple is depicted on the modern Egyptian LE 50 note **(11)**. In the temple at Edfu there is a picture of Ptolemy being crowned by the Goddesses of northern and southern Egypt and this is shown on the LE 20 note **(12)**. However on that note the picture is very small, so the original picture from within the temple is reproduced **(12a)**. Incidental this picture on the LE 20 note **(12)** is the only portrait of a Ptolemy on any twentieth century currency of Egypt. Ptolemy III was very active militarily. During his reign Egypt reached its zenith as an international power.

Ptolemy III was followed by his son, Ptolemy IV who was a weak ruler, and a devotee of Serapis and Isis and issued a coin portraying them **(13)**. The latter's son Ptolemy V was only five years of age when his father died and the country was initially in the hands of incompetent ministers and several of Egypt's foreign possessions were lost. For his coronation the stele which we know as the Rosetta stone was inscribed, in Greek, Demotic and Hieroglyphics, leading to the deciphering of the latter. Ptolemy V married Cleopatra I.

Ptolemy VI although initially a joint ruler with his younger brother, another Ptolemy (who eventually became Ptolemy VIII), quarrelled with him. Rome, acting as arbitrator, split the domain, giving Egypt to Ptolemy VI and Cyrenia to his brother. The two eagles on the coin **(14)** may be symbolic of the early joint rule of the brothers. Ptolemy VI also issued coins portraying his mother Cleopatra I shown as Isis **(15)**. Further south down the Nile he built a new temple at Kom Ombo. The Nile is of course the source of life in Egypt. Within this temple at Kom Ombo, Hapi the Nile god is depicted, bearing gifts, along with one of Ptolemy's titles, 'Autocrat'. This picture is shown on the current LE 5 note **(16)**, along with this title in hieroglyphics, which are detailed in the Appendix.

Rulers, at this stage of the dynasty, squabbled, married incestuously and were involved in co-rulerships. For example Ptolemy VI was followed briefly – for one year - by his son Ptolemy VII, who was murdered by Ptolemy VIII, who married his sister, who was also his brother's widow. Ptolemy VIII then ruled for about three decades. Later Ptolemy X **(18)**, the younger son of Ptolemy VIII, ousted his older brother Ptolemy IX from the throne and ruled jointly with his mother.

Ptolemy XII, following the example of his predecessors, made improvements to many temples, including Philae. A picture of him, slaying his enemies, can be seen on the major pylon at Philae which is depicted on an old LE 1 note **(19)**. During his reign the tetradrachm declined from fourteen to eleven grams and was slightly debased. His daughter Cleopatra VII succeeded him.

Cleopatra VII (the famous Cleopatra) initially became joint ruler with her brothers Ptolemy XIII, and then Ptolemy XIV. Her liaisons with Julius Caesar and Mark Antony are well known and needn't be repeated here. Suffice it to note she had a son, Ptolemy XV, by Caesar and she eventually married Mark Antony.

Her tetradrachms became increasingly debased during her reign, during which some of them contained less than 50 percent silver. These still portrayed Ptolemy I, but she issued some bronze coins with her portrait, e.g. an obol **(20).** This, obol on the reverse, had the usual eagle, but also the title *ΚΛΕΟΠΑΤΡΑΣ ΒΑΣΙΛΙΣΣΗΣ* (Queen Cleopatra) and a mark indicating its value.

General features of the Ptolemaic coinage

Turning to the subject of coins in general - rather than issues of specific rulers, it is useful initially to recall comments in the preface.

When the Egyptian domain was very large it would have been sensible to mint coins in distant provinces for use in these provinces rather than mint them in Egypt itself and then have to transport them thousands of miles. So for example some Ptolemaic coins were minted in Tyre and Sidon **(8).** Also while Egypt had good sources of gold, it has always been short of silver. So if its territory included places with good silver sources, it would be sensible to mint coins there. Cyprus had richer sources of silver than Egypt and many Ptolemaic tetradrachms were minted in Cyprus at for example Paphos and Salamis, with appropriate mint marks. Nowadays Cyprus sees these coins as part of its numismatic past, which was illustrated on a series of Cypriot stamps, which was issued in 1977.

As noted earlier, the Egyptian coinage was a closed currency. This is seen from hoard evidence already from the time of Ptolemy I. A papyrus of 258/7 B. C. indicates a process used to maintain this: people coming from abroad with foreign gold coins had to exchange them for Ptolemaic gold at the mint. A similar procedure was also applied to incoming silver coins.

In most modern currencies coins bear a date which is related to a specific era, for example our coin dates are of the Christian era. In the early Egyptian coinages they had no such era. (The Ptolemy rulers attempted to set up such an era, starting with Ptolemy I, but it faded out). Eventually both Ptolemaic and Roman coins in Egypt used regnal dates i.e. a coin would have on it a figure indicating the year, of the reign of the ruler who produced it, in which the coin was issued,. These figures would actually be the Greek letters which were used as numerals for numbers in Greek, as listed in the Appendix. These were often preceded by the letter L, as a symbol for 'year'. For a later roman example see the coin of Vespasian (25) where the date is LA i.e. Year 1.

The introduction of money into Ptolemaic Egypt had several functions in addition to its basic economic one. Among early Greek states there was a degree of competitiveness in asserting civic identity. Coinage has an important political role in this. Coins were one of the best means of communication available. The coinage propagates the notion of a state as a discrete entity to its citizens and to neighbouring states. In Egypt it increased the political integration of the disparate groups in the Nile valley. However although the coinage helped unify different regions of the country, the population remained stratified, with different social classes of people. Most of the Ptolemy rulers, who were of Greek descent, did not speak Egyptian.

Not only did the coinage put forward ideas about the state, it propagated ideas about the rulers. In some of its designs the coinage merged Greek and Egyptian ideas of the monarch. The Greeks saw their rulers as kings. In Egypt the ruler, the pharaoh, was perceived as a god. On coins generally Ptolemy was described as King, but on some early Ptolemaic gold coins there were suggestions of divinity. When Arsinoe II died she was proclaimed a goddess and a cult of Arsinoe, to be celebrated in all temples, was established. To help propagate this Ptolemy II issued a gold Octodrachm, on which divine attributes were included, for Arsinoe wears a crown with the lotus tip of a sceptre above and a small horn of Ammon by her ear. For a portrait of Arsinoe see item (37). For other divine attributions on an impressive coin of Ptolemy II, which depicts conjoined busts of his parents, there is the title *ΘΕΩΝ*, 'the Gods'. Later on, a gold coin portraying Ptolemy III shows him wearing the radiant crown of Helios, and the aegis of Zeus, and carrying the trident of Poseidon, suggesting he had attributes of these Gods. In view of the military and naval successes he achieved, these attributes were perhaps not undeserved.

The coins of different metals were used in different sections of society. Gold was used among the upper classes for donations and special rewards, as a store of wealth and for very large payments, for example to the military. The silver coinage was used mainly in the Alexandrian region and for international trade. It was hardly ever used in the Nile valley where, in the countryside, bronze coins were the currency in use. Local wages and goods were paid for in bronze coins. At least from the time of Ptolemy II there was a monetary poll-tax to be paid by all adults throughout the country and it was paid in bronze. There were also other taxes, but a noteworthy one was a sort of tithe to support the cult of Arsinoe on vineyards and orchards – a sixth of their produce had to be paid ultimately to the temples (von Reden, 2010).

3

THE ROMAN ALEXANDRIAN COINS

Background

After Antony married Cleopatra, they eventually confronted Octavian at the battle of Actium, which they lost. They fled back to Alexandria and finally committed suicide, and so Octavian in effect conquered Egypt. When he took over Egypt in 30 B.C. there were there coins of the ptolemaic series, which in its final years consisted of very debased tetradrachms and bronze coins. The Romans continued to use these ptolemaic coins in Egypt until the reign of Trajan. These Alexandrian coins differed from the normal roman imperial currency, in that they had greek script like some other roman provincial coins, which are sometimes called 'Greek Imperial'. The basic silver coins, tetradrachms, were billon, i.e. silver mixed with copper. These Alexandrian coins were not used outside Egypt.

The Roman series

In 30 B.C., with ptolemaic coins still circulating, Octavian, (later called Augustus), had minted in Egypt only bronze coins: an obol **(21)** and its fractions. These coins initially copied the type of that of Cleopatra; with a portrait obverse and eagle reverse. Perhaps as has been suggested by Milne (1971), Octavian had thought that for the silver coins, the roman denarii used throughout the Empire, could be used for external trade. Tiberius reintroduced the debased tetradrachms **(22)** in about 20 AD. These were of irregular weight but contained about the same amount of silver as a denarius. He continued to issue bronze coins.

The tetradrachms were issued regularly by emperors over the next three centuries although few emperors visited the country. Nero had planned to visit Egypt but did not get there before his suicide. He had led a very extravagant life and so to recoup funds he, among other things, debased the coinage of the Empire including that of Egypt. Even so he enlarged and extensively developed the Alexandrian coinage. Besides the normal imperial portraits and occasional Egyptian items, e.g. hippopotami etc., he issued many coins showing Greek and Egyptian gods.

In addition, he had minted in Alexandria a series of coins referring to his single trip abroad **(23)**. He had travelled to Greece and, being a keen musician, participated in musical festivals and competitions there. The series of coins depicted the patron gods of these festivals at Olympia, Delphi and Corinth etc., the latter being represented by Poseidon Isthmus **(24)**. The output of his Alexandrian coinage was huge: more than half the tetradrachms circulating in Egypt in the next 100 years were minted in his last four years from 64 to 68 AD., when he committed suicide.

Following his death various people fought for the throne. Vespasian was proclaimed Emperor in Alexandria by his troops in 69 A.D. In that year he was still fighting for the throne, so his first tetradrachms, **(25)** show a personification of 'Alexandria' offering a victor's wreath and another lauding peace. He also issued in that first year a copper coin depicting the god Nilus. Later Hadrian toured the country and Septimius Severus also paid a brief visit, so for both of these there were coins showing 'Alexandria' greeting the Emperor e.g. **(26)**. During Hadrian's stay in Egypt, his favourite youth Antinoos was drowned. This caused him great grief and his adoration of the youth led him to found the town of Antinoopolis (Sheikh el Ibada) on the Nile. He encouraged countries of the Empire to honour, indeed deify, Antinoos and so many coins were issued depicting him, including some from Alexandria **(27)**.

Roman Alexandrian coins incidentally provide a good source of imperial portraits. Of all the various groups of people who have ruled Egypt, we know the most about the early roman emperors because of the details provided in classical literature. We know about their lives in general and how they as individuals thought about themselves, i.e. about their self-identities. Details of some of these thoughts about themselves are reflected in some of the Alexandrian series coins.

For example Nero, as noted above was very fond of music and had remarked 'Singing is sacred to Apollo' (Tacitus, Annals). In the Alexandrian coinage he shows his reverence for Apollo by depicting him in several forms on the coins **(28)**.

Other emperors exhibited more normal aspects of imperial life. Domitian, for instance, who had always felt he had had to play second best to his father and older brother in their military celebrations, after his military successes in Germany proudly displayed his title Germanicus, 'ΓΕΡΜ(ΩΝ)' on his Alexandrian coins, as well as on his imperial coins.

Coins of course do not tell us about the illness of emperors but they sometimes tell us what they did to try to alleviate illness. Thus Hadrian, who in his later years suffered badly – perhaps from heart trouble, appealed to Aesculapius, the god of healing, for help, as is seen on some of his medalions (32) and coins, including an Alexandrian one on which the god is shown in the same standing posture as on the medalion.

Marcus Aurelius, although of a studious, philosophical disposition, unfortunately had to spend most of his time fighting wars in the north. He did this from a sense of duty to the Empire. While friends had told him he could leave wars to his generals and live in comfort at Rome, he considered 'Where ever a man has placed himself, he should stay and abide the hazard taking nothing into reckoning, either death or anything, rather than desert his post' (Marcus Aurelius, 'Meditations'). We see him on one of the Alexandrian coins on horseback with some of his soldiers.

Incidentally he is the only Roman emperor represented on a modern coin: he is seen on an Italian coin, a 50 cent Euro coin, similarly riding a horse.

Sometimes emperors had deluded views of themselves. Commodus believed he was Hercules reincarnated and had given orders he should he called Hercules (Herodian). He is seen on one Alexandrian coin depicted as that god.

Finally Septimius Severus is a rare Emperor who records his victories in Britain on his Alexandrian coinage, 'NEIKH KATA BPET' (Victory over Britain). He is also an example of some emperors who gave considerable significance to their family.

On one Alexandrian coin, he portrays his wife on the obverse and his two sons, Caracalla and Geta, on the reverse. On his deathbed he had told his sons 'Be harmonious with each other,..enrich the soldiers' (Hadas 1958). Unfortunately the first part of this advice was ignored. Soon after Caracalla killed his brother Geta.

Besides telling us about emperors, the series of coins also illustrates the hair styles of empresses, as do some of the imperial coinage.

(These sketches illustrate hair styles, they do not portray the actual empresses.)

Poppaea	Plotina	Faustina II	Julia Domna	Severina
50 AD	100AD	150AD	200AD	270AD

These hairstyles were copied by well-to-do ladies throughout the empire, including some in Egypt. Some of the latter, Egyptian ladies, are illustrated on the Faiyum portraits. These are portraits of the deceased painted on mummies etc. in the early roman period. Many of these have been found in the Faiyum region of Egypt (cf. illustrations in Doxiadis).

The series of coins also illustrates busts of Egyptian gods; e.g. the Nile as on a coin of Trajan (29) and the new god Serapis (30), and related items, e.g. the personification of Alexandria (31). It does not show much of Egypt itself. The only definitely identified building illustrated is the Pharos lighthouse, one of the wonders of the ancient world, which no longer exists. Other buildings on the coins like temples were probably standard designs not specific buildings, with perhaps one exception, noted below.

The bronze coinage, started by Augustus and continued by Tiberius, developed into the second century, by then there was a series of six bronze coins, from minute, rare chalkons (27), through obels (21) to large coins which were equivalent to the imperial sestertius. These large coins provided opportunities for attractive and interesting designs such as one illustrating,for example the Pharos lighthouse (33), and Antoninus Pius produced a series exhibiting the signs of the zodiac (34). Marcus Aurelius issued a coin which Sear suggest shows the Caesarium (35). This was an important building in Alexandria of which only rubble remains so unfortunately it is not known what it really looked like. After Marcus Aurelius the production of bronze coinage decreased and eventually disappeared except for occasional ceremonial coins. Nevertheless for internal local use at about this time, there were also other often small coins **(37)** of copper and/or lead issued by the local nomes – i.e. administrative districts (de Rouge & Feuardent 1979).

Towards the end of the third century, Diocletian, realising that controlling a huge Empire was almost too much for one person, promoted a general, Maximianus **(36),** to be a co-augustus and then later two others to be co-rulers, caesars, thus establishing a Tetrarchy.

He reformed the general imperial coinage, which was experiencing a considerable inflation; among other things he introduced the follis **(40)**, with 240 folles to the aureus. Another of Diocletian's major administrative moves was to end the distinctive Alexandrian coinage in 296 A.D. During the last 75 years of this coinage, it consisted only of debased tetradrachms. These billon tetradrachms, as noted earlier, had greek legends and could be used only in Egypt. The Alexandrian mint then, in 296 A.D., started issuing imperial coins like those used in the rest of the empire. They had latin legends. So for a few years for Diocletian and his colleagues, there was an overlap, there being both tetradrachms and imperial coins from that mint in circulation.

For example two such coins of Maximianus are illustrated, **(36)** and **(39).**

During his reign Diocletian faced many rebellions and for a brief period in 296 a usurper Domitius Domitianus was proclaimed emperor in Alexandria and issued there three denominations of coins, double, single and half tetradrachms, but these are rare and the rebellion was soon defeated. A column in Alexandria celebrates this defeat. Diocletian visited Egypt after this rebellion, being the last roman emperor to visit there. While there, he had built at the fortress of Babylon in Old Cairo two defensive towers. One is still there, a church stands on the site of the other. More generally he is perhaps best known for his later persecution of Christians, including those in Egypt.

General aspects of the coinage

The coins continued to exhibit the regnal date system started in the ptolemaic coinage. For example see the illustration of the coin of Vespasian **(25)** where the A, in LA, indicates year 1. Sometimes, particularly on the large bronze coins, the regnal year is written in words, as for example on the Antoninus Pius coin **(33)** where 'twelve' is written in greek, as is seen in the 'Key'.

When considering an old coin, one often wonders exactly what it was worth to the local population when it was in circulation. What were the Roman Alexandrian coins of the first two centuries worth in daily use? In the early first century the daily wage for digging was 3 obols, i.e a half drachm. Across the second century, this day wage for digging had risen to 7 to 10 obols. In the first century a 1lb loaf cost 1 to 2 obols, while the hire of a donkey for a day cost about 5 obols. In the second century such a loaf cost 4 obols, while a day hire of a donkey cost about 10 obols, although a donkey cost on average about 200 drachms. (Duncan Jones1994). (Prices in Egypt were somewhat lower than corresponding ones in Italy and especially those in Rome).

The imperial roman coinage, often had a considerable propaganda role. Coins told the world, particularly the people of Rome, about the Emperors, their victories, how thy helped stricken provinces etc., and how beneficial they were in Rome: creating fine public buildings, giving out largess, looking after orphans etc. The Alexandrian coins presented only a limited view of this. They broadcast victories, but as the Emperors were not inclined to be beneficial to the population of Egypt, there were few of the positive deeds eulogised by the imperial coinage

The roman Alexandrian tetradrachm series provides a good example of the decline and demise of a coin, as is illustrated by the graph in the appendix. An early tetradrachm had roughly the same silver content as a denarius and was equivalent to it in value (Sear 2000). Under Tiberius **(22)** tetradrachms started briefly at 30 – 40 percent silver, but rapidly were reduced to about 20 percent under Claudius. The silver content, like that of the denarius, was then slowly further reduced. It was debased by Nero to about 16 percent and "this standard was maintained over 100 years" (Walker 1974). It was then reduced under Commodus **(38)** to about 7 percent, which standard also continued for a century, and later to about 2 percent by the time of Claudius II and then almost to zero. The silver reduction in the tetradrachms was more rapid than that in the denarii. By the time of Commodus the silver content of the tetradrachm was only a third of that in the denarius. In size tetradrachms remained about the same weight, thirteen to ten grams, for a couple of centuries, until about the time of Gallienus and Valerian II, and then rapidly reduced to on average six to seven grams, (although there was a wide variation around this), until it was ended by Diocletian and the other members of the tetrarchy, Constantius I, etc., in 296 AD. Thus while the weight did not change much early on, the silver content did. This is seen if one compares e.g. coins of the adjacent reigns of Marcus Aurelius and Commodus **(38)**.

How was all this debasement seen by the people of the time? Ancient writers say little about currency changes and there seems to have been little awareness of such changes (Duncan Jones 1994). When a currency was debased by a small amount the population did not react strongly. Larger debasements however produced more public reaction. There was the steep debasement in the Alexandrian coinage in the third century and this produced problems of confidence due to the difference between older and newer coins – all of which were equal in nominal value. It seems that e.g. people operating banks of exchange were not willing to accept the newer coins. This necessitated an official injunction being issued to them and to all others engaged in business transactions to accept them or suffer the ordained penalties (Burnett 1987). A further reaction to a debasement in the time of Justinian is noted in the next section.

Finally it perhaps is worth noting there were no gold coins minted in Alexandria. This may be related to the contrast noted in the Preface. Ptolemaic Egypt was an independent state aiming at self-sufficiency. Anything it wanted it had to provide itself and so it had to mint its own gold coins. However under the Romans Egypt was merely an attachment to a well organised empire, which produced gold coins at many major mints. Gold coins were used in Egypt only very rarely. Any gold coins needed there at the time could be easily imported from well established western mints of the Empire.

4

THE CHRISTIAN PERIOD AND THE BYZANTINE EMPIRE

This period is initially the same in time as that covered by the previous section of this work, but it is looked at from a different viewpoint.

The development of Christianity in Egypt

To put the next development of the coinage into context, we recall that in the early days of the Christian era the family of Christ fled south into Egypt to avoid Herod's slaughter of infants. One of the reasons for their choosing Egypt - rather than elsewhere - was probably because there was a large and prosperous Jewish community there. Christ's family travelled in Egypt and nowadays there is a well known route that some pilgrims make following their journey, there being a series of churches at the places at which they are reputed to have stayed. In Old Cairo, for instance, there is the church of St Sergius, where they are supposed to have stayed in a cave which is now the crypt.

A few decades later, when Christianity was developing, Saint Mark visited Egypt, preaching and consolidating the religion there. In the early centuries there were various persecutions of christians and the last major one was by Diocletian. Shortly after Diocletian's death one of his corulers, Galerius issued the Edict of Toleration, in 311 A.D. Later the substance of that Edict was confirmed by Constantine in the Edict of Milan. These Edicts allowed freedom of worship and at last a person could be both a good Roman and a Christian. In Egypt the church which developed there was granted its own patriarch by the Council of Nicea in 325.

Returning to the coinage, from the middle of the third century for the next 150 years there was a serious inflation in the general imperial currency. Diocletian tried to control it with a Price Edict, which set the prices for all goods, this did not succeed. After Diocletian's abolition of the Alexandrian tetradrachms etc. in 296 A.D., ordinary imperial coins were issued in Egypt, i.e. the mint now used latin inscriptions not greek ones. By this time the original roman denominations, the denarius, sestertius etc., were no longer used and had been replaced by the antoninianus, argenteus, follis and later the centenionalis. Some were minted in Alexandria with the 'ALE' mintmark in the exergue **(40)**. This change from the unique Alexandrian coins to the use of imperial coins is significant. Previously the Alexandrian coins were a closed coinage; they were restricted to Egypt where the general imperial coins were not used. After this date Egypt used the same coins as the rest of the Empire.

Shortly afterwards Constantine the Great, after he had consolidated his grip on the Empire, founded Constantinople as its eastern capital (about 330). He had also become Christian and by law-making and building churches etc., facilitated the development of Christianity. After his death commemorative coins were issued, including some from Alexandria **(41)** and his new capital Constantinople. After that some coins were issued bearing Christian symbols. The most common was the Chi-Rho, the first two letters of Christ's name in Greek. This commonly occurred on a labarum, a banner carried by a soldier or an Emperor e.g. Constans **(42)**. Besides this symbol, some later coins exhibited simply the cross. Some of these coins with a Christian symbol were minted in Alexandria. Among other changes to the coins, Constantine introduced the gold solidus (1/72 lbs, that is 4.4 grams) which eventually replaced the Aureus (1/60 lbs) as the main gold coin. Gold became the standard, the most stable part of the currency for the next few centuries. As noted at the end of the last section, some gold coins were taken into Egypt for use there. For instance, Fakhry in his excavations of old Coptic villages in the Bahriyah oasis (Ahmed Fakhry 1974) found, along with some jewellery, a gold coin of Valens **(43)**. These items are deposited in the Coptic museum in Cairo.

In 392 the Emperor Theodosius prohibited pagan worship throughout the Empire. Hence Christianity was established as the official religion in the Empire, including Egypt. For about the next two and a half centuries from this date Christianity was the official religion of Egypt. This increased the tendency among Christians there to deface the statues of the old gods in Egyptian temples, which they closed– as pagan

In the early days of Christianity there were many theological controversies. One dispute concerned the nature of Christ. The Monophysites argued that Christ has only one nature, that is that he is divine. This was debated during the reign of Marcian at the Council of Chalcedon, 451 A.D., which concluded that he has two natures and that Monophysitism was a heresy. Nevertheless the Egyptian church continued to maintain the Monophysitic doctrine. This led to oppression and persecution of the Egyptians by, and hence their hostility towards, the orthodox Christians of Constantinople. These and other disputes led to rifts within the church worldwide. Eventually the Egyptian (Coptic) church, with its own patriarch (Pope) split off from its mother church based at Constantinople, which was already separate from the church of Rome. The modern Coptic church still adheres to Monophysitism and thereby differs from the rest of Christendom. The title Coptic is from the greek word (gyptios) for Egyptian.

The evolution of the Eastern Empire into the Byzantine Empire

In 395, after the death of Theodosius, the Roman Empire split with Honorius ruling the west and Arcadius ruling the eastern half, which included Egypt. The capital of the eastern half was Constantinople, which had previously been called Byzantium. While the Empire was thus split, both Emperors were represented by coins in both halves, e.g. coins were issued by Arcadius both in his own name with the ALE mintmark, Ae 11, **(44)** and in the name of Honorius. The eastern half eventually became known as the Byzantine Empire. Initially this still used roman imperial coins, which eventually consisted mainly of gold coins, a few silver and copper coins which, because of inflation, became smaller and smaller, eventually becoming tiny coins called nummi. These were very small, about nine mm in diameter, with a solidus exchanging at one stage for about 6000 nummi.

However in the fifth century, in the reign of Marcian, the authorities in Constantinople were in dispute with the Egyptians, as just noted, Marcian himself being a strong enforcer of the Chalcedon doctrine. Marcian did not mint coins in Alexandria, indeed most Emperors did not mint coins in Alexandria and so very few 'Egyptian coins' were produced, most coins in Egypt coming from Constantinople.

However in 498 in the reign of Anastasius the coinage was reformed and distinctive coins, later called byzantine coins, were issued. These eventually had greek numerals and script instead of the traditional latin ones. The Byzantine Empire was strongly Christian and this was reflected in its coins, as in noted below. Byzantine coins were issued from many mints in the eastern empire and typically each mint's coins would include gold solidi and fractions thereof, silver miliaresia and siliquae and copper coins. The latter usually consisted of large folles – marked with a capital M (one follis being equal 40 nummi, M being greek for 40), half folles marked with K (= 20 nummi, K being greek for 20 etc), quarters with I (=10) called decanummia, and pentanummia, with E (=5). Most of these circulated widely in the Byzantine Empire. Early on, in the time of Justinian, one solidus equalled 180 folles. However these copper coins quickly decreased in value and size. Particularly in the reign of Heraclius the follis decreased in weight from about 10 gms to about 5gms. While some of these circulated in Egypt, usually the only copper coins actually minted in Egypt, during the reigns of the nine Byzantine Emperors who ruled before the Arabs took over Egypt, were small copper coins of unique denominations of twelve or six or three nummi. The IB on the illustrated twelve nummi coin, a duodecanummia, **(45)** is greek for twelve. It is likely the unit of twelve nummi was chosen as the coin's size and value represented those of surviving billon tetradrachms (Grierson 1982). It is noteworthy that the obverse legend is in latin and the reverse script is in greek. Initially 3 twelve nummi coins were equal about one follis. However with the general weight decline of the imperial follis, it seems that at one stage "the Egyptian duodecanummia had the same value as the follis elsewhere, the 2 coins being virtually the same weight" (Grierson). On the small coins the only major changes in type occurred when Heraclius and his successors replaced the traditional profile **(46)** bust with facing busts, i.e. busts facing 'out' of the coin rather than sideways. Usually in the case of Heraclius there were two busts (not one): i.e. himself and his son **(47)**. The one exception to this series of small copper coins minted in Alexandria was a thirty three nummi coin issued by Justinian. In addition to the small copper coins, three emperors minted solidi in Alexandria, but these are very rare, and so for many large transactions in Egypt solidi from the rest of the empire must have been brought into the country. For example a large collection of several hundred solidi from the reigns of Phocus and Heraclius, was found in the St. Shenoute monastery at Sohag. These are now in the Coptic museum. Concerning the contemporary value of the coinage, around the time of Phocus, about 600 A.D., a manual worker earned about five folles per day, i.e. ten solidi per year. The cost of food varied, but early in the sixth century the median cost of wheat was one solidus for twelve artebas (with one arteba equal 1.1 bushels). One arteba would yield about 80 lbs of bread. That is 80 lbs of bread cost a twelfth of a solidus i.e. fifteen folles. So one follis purchased about 5.3 lbs bread. So the unique Egyptian coin, a twelve nummi coin would initially buy a loaf of about one and a half lb., but later in the last decade of Heraclius perhaps 2. (Banaji 2001. Johnson & West 1949).

As the Byzantine Empire was strongly Christian, most of the small Egyptian Byzantine coins ever since the time of Anastasius had a cross on them (continuing the practice noted earlier. As the Copts were prominent at the time, some Egyptian dealers nowadays call them coptic coins, although they are of course not specifically coptic. One shown here **(45)** is of Justinian I who in his long reign greatly enhanced many aspects of the empire, including the building of the magnificent St Sophia in Constantinople. Incidentally Justinian undertook an immense building programme, both in Constantinople and elsewhere. This extravagance led to financial problems. At one stage, to increase his income he debased the coinage, but this led to riots and so he had to restore the coins to their original value

In the early church in Egypt an important innovation was the establishment of monasteries. This initiated the development of Christian monasticism worldwide. One of the most important monasteries in Egypt is that of St Catherine founded by Justinian in 527 on Sinai. St Catherine was an early Christian martyred in Alexandria under Maxentius (306 – 312 A.D.). Monasteries and churches are the main buildings left from this period.

In the region generally the Byzantine Empire was often under attack on many sides. In the east the Persians under Khusru II were invading and conquering parts of the empire. Jerusalem was captured and the Persian took away relics including 'the True Cross'. In 619 they conquered Egypt and had minted there the usual twelve nummi coin but with the addition of a star and crescent, which were symbols on Khusru's Persian coinage, on either side of a facing portrait **(48)**.

Some these are a lot thicker than the traditional byzantine coins **(49)**. Fortunately for the Byzantine Empire, which at that time seemed about to disintegrate, just as the Western Roman Empire was doing, there arose one of its greatest leaders, Heraclius. He eventually defeated the Persians in 629, recapturing Egypt. He also rescued the 'True Cross' and returned it to Jerusalem.

Unfortunately, while Heraclius strengthened the core of the empire, he was old and eventually the empire was attacked by a new power. The Muslims conquered outlying parts of the Empire, including different parts of Egypt in 641 and 642, which they have held ever since.

Egypt is nowadays mainly Islamic but Copts form about ten per cent of the population. As Copts tend to marry other Copts they may be seen as descendents of some of the original inhabitants of Egypt. Although they live throughout Egypt they are found in higher proportions in the south, and there is a large coptic cathedral there in Aswan.

5

THE COMING OF THE ARABS

When the Romans and then the Byzantines ruled Egypt, they did so from their distant well established capitals. They used existing towns as administrative bases and did not erect many major new cities. They did not attempt to colonise the country Before the islamic invasion, there were already nomadic Arabs in Egypt. After the arab conquest waves of immigrant Arabs came in and settled there.

The rise of Islam and the development of Islamic Cairo

The Arabs had been a nomadic people. Islam emerged as a world religion when Mohammed fled from Mecca in 622 A.D. Mohammed grew up in a community (Ishaq) which worshiped many gods, although in the region there were Jewish and Christian communities whose monotheistic ideas he would have encountered. Periodically he withdrew from society to meditate and he had revelations from God. Later he had a divine command to proclaim what had been revealed to him. His preaching led to opposition and he fled from Mecca to Medina where he found more appreciative hearers, some of whom became his followers (Ishaq 1964). In the ensuing decades the new religion spread rapidly as Mohammed and his followers conquered surrounding lands; Syria etc. Mohammed's work was carried on by his successors, the Caliphs (this word is derived from the arabic for 'successor'). A general, Amr, of one of the earliest Caliphs, Umar, conquered Egypt in 640 and founded Fustat at a site which later became Cairo. The early Caliphs had Damascus as their main capital. From among the earliest major line of Caliphs, the Umayyads, a couple, Marwan I & II, visited Egypt (Lane Poole 1901). The Umayyads were replaced in 750 A.D by the Abbasids who eventually made Baghdad their capital. These were all mainstream Moslems, called Sunnis. The driving force behind Islam was the nomad, some early mosques exemplified desert architecture often involving 'a walled defensive enclosure around a well' (Rawson 1966). Examples of these occurred widely from e.g. Qairawan in Tunis to Samarra in Iraq. During the Abbasid caliphate a governor of Egypt, Ahmad ibn Tulun, built a mosque, when Fustat was not strongly protected. His mosque was erected like a square fort. It was built around a well, for ablutions, and also incorporated a minaret. Ibn Tulun's successors, semiautonomous governors of Egypt the Tulunids, were followed in 935 for about three decades by the Ikhshidids.

Cairo is usually considered to have been founded, as 'al Qahira' (the Victorious), in 969 by the Fatimids, when they conquered Egypt from the Ikhshidids. They adhered to a rival sect of Islam, the Shi'ites, (this name is derived from a word meaning 'a sect') who are ideologically opposed to the mainstream Sunnis. One of their first acts in building Cairo was to erect a mosque – the al Azhar. Later in the reign of Aziz, the Azhar was developed to include a collegiate school, which is perhaps the world's most important school for the study of Islam. Much later in the nineteenth century, this school was developed into a university. In the reign of Mustansir, who, ruling for about 60 years, was one of the longest reigning Mohammedan caliphs, the Fatimids, in about 1060 A.D., erected walls with massive gates to defend the city. During his reign Egypt suffered a terrible 7 year famine.

Later Egypt was taken over by the Ayyubids, members of the orthodox Sunni branch of Islam. Their leader Salah - ad – din, known generally as Saladin, established the brief dynasty of Ayyubids. Originally a general and vassal of the ruler of Syria, when he took over Egypt from the Fatimids he was acting on behalf of that ruler and the Sunni Abbasid Caliph of Baghdad. There were two lines of caliphs at this time: the Fatimids in Cairo and the Abbasids in Baghdad. When Saladin ousted the Fatimids, the Abbasid Caliph invested him as Lord of Egypt. Hereafter Ayyubid rulers were entitled Malik (King) on their coins, as were the Mamluks who followed them. Saladin's dynasty in Egypt ended, 1250, about the same time as the Abbasid Caliphate. This ended when Mongols sacked Baghdad and the Caliph was assassinated in 1258. During the Ayyubid period, Cairo was greatly enlarged and the citadel was built in 1179. The Ayyubids under Saladin developed some mosques into collegiate mosques, by introducing a cruciform ground plan, to accommodate the teaching of the four rites of orthodox Islam.

The Ayyubids like many Islamic dynasties of the time used slave troops. Some of these the Mamluks ('Mamluk' means 'slave') eventually took over from their masters After the fall of the Caliphate at Bagdad, a survivor of the Caliph's family was invited by the Mamluks to Cairo and was invested there as Caliph. He then gave the Mamluk leader the title of 'Sultan' (i.e. ruler) which the Mamluks thereafter put on their coins. During this period of the Ayyubids and Mamluks considerable financial development took place in Egypt which became central to east-west trade between Europe and India. Of course trade by itself does not enrich the government of a country. To do this the government imposes taxes on the trade. With regard to tax in general, rulers of this period taxed land and the raw produce thereof. They taxed industries, e.g. the manufacture of linen, and copper items etc., and property. They often had a poll tax on non-Moslems, this poll tax varied but averaged about two dinars per year. The majority of payers of this tax were Copts, along with a number of Jews. Incidentally the tax on the Copts led to some Copts 'converting' to Islam to avoid having to pay the tax and so the Copt population slowly decreased. Internally this taxation in general led to great artistic and architectural developments. The first mosque on the Citadel, the al Nasir Mohammed, and the mosques of Qalawoun and Sultan Hasan, both of which exhibit a cruciform plan (as shown in the appendix), and the tombs of the Mamluks, e.g. of Kait Bay, are good examples of such developments. Besides architecture these caliphs, particularly al Nasir, patronised small arts: beautiful copperware, fine furniture, enamelled glass lamps etc.. In the following century there was fear of invasion by the Ottomans, a growing power in the north, and various Sultans built defensive forts, for example Kait Bay built one to defend Alexandria in 1477 on the spot where the Pharos lighthouse had been. This lighthouse had collapsed following earthquakes in 1303 onwards.

About this time the prosperous central trade position of Egypt decreased in importance due to, for example, the development of a trade route around the Cape of Good Hope in 1498. The Mamluk economy was deteriorating due to these and other trade problems, and the extravagance of the ruling classes and the cost of wars.

The coins

Initially the Arabs used the coins of the different people they conquered, the Byzantines, Sassanians etc., often just with an Arabic inscription added. Like most coins up to this time, these coins usually had pictorial designs on them. In 696 however Abd el Malik reformed the coinage so that, in line with Islamic doctrine, there were no pictorial designs (e.g. ruler's portraits) on the coins just statements. There was a religious message, the Kalima: 'There is no God but Allah, he is alone and has no partner' cf (52). There was also an inscription – which starts 'In the name of God' -the Bismillah - which also stated the coin's value, date of issue and sometimes where it was minted. Arab dates start from 622 A.D., i.e. Mohammed's flight. Later the Abbasids placed on the reverse of coins the second part of the Kalima, 'Mohammed is the messenger of Allah' (51). (For the Arabic for these expressions and the dating system, see the Appendix). This coin type remained the basis of islamic coins, which propagated the main tenets of Islam, for centuries.

In the early Umayyad and Abbasid periods Egypt had no indigenous coins. The earliest Islamic coins in Egypt; gold dinars and silver dirhems, were imported from Syria etc. These early dinars, based on the Byzantine solidus (the denarius aureus), were typically 4.25 grams in weight. The dirhems were about 2.95 grams. The earliest indigenous Islamic Egyptian coins were copper fulus, some in the time of Marwen II, about 740 A.D., some of which were inscribed with the name of the local Umayyad finance minister (50). Eventually the Abbasids also produced dirhems and dinars (51) and (52) in Egypt and so all three denominations were minted there. Ma'mun (52), was the first Abbasid caliph to visit Egypt. Under the Abbasids a dinar was worth twelve to twenty dirhems, although the exchange rate varied over time and in different provinces, depending for example on the availability of gold and silver.

The format of the coins slowly evolved. To the initial basic items noted above were added the Caliph's name and eventually the names of Governors of specific regions, when they felt independent enough. Thus a coin then proclaimed a dual power structure: recording the spiritual authority of the Caliph and the secular local authority of the Governor. For example the local Governor Ahmad ibn Tulun (54) and his son Khumarawayh (54a) both issued coins, each with his own name and that of the current Caliph Al Mu'tamid (54), (54a). In addition while initially there was one marginal legend around the Kalima, eventually there were two as on the illustrations of the coins of the Caliph Muqtadir (53) and the Tulunids (54). (For the layout of the various names on the coins, see the comments in the "Key to currency illustrations" concerning coins **(54)** & **(54a)**). While most Ikhshidid coins were similar in format to their predecessors **(55)**, their coinage included a couple of unusual features. Firstly they issued some rare presentation pieces depicting human figures. Secondly some of their coin inscriptions included the letter Kaf the initial letter of Kafer, a black Abyssinian eunuch who governed Egypt briefly within the Ikhshidid period (Bacharach 2006).

When the Fatimids conquered Egypt in 969, their coins had inscriptions which were often arranged in concentric circles, so they are sometimes called 'bull's eye' coins **(56)** & **(57)**. Their coins were mainly of gold, silver being quite scarce. Initially their dinars were of high quality gold of which they at first had good sources: mines in West Africa and Nubia and even gold taken from the tombs of Pharaohs. Also Egyptian trade flourished at this time. They also issued fractional dinars. Gradually their gold supplies diminished. Some of their early dinars were worth 15 ½ dirhems. Although as Egypt was chronically short of silver, the dirhem, always rare in Egypt, was eventually reduced both in weight and fineness. At one stage thirty or more dirhems exchanged for one dinar. They minted no copper coins in Egypt, but produced coin sized glass weights which were probably used as a token currency.

The Shi'ite Fatimids were ousted by Saladin **(58),** who founded the Ayyubid dynasty which eventually ruled a large area of the Middle East, with different regions being ruled by different members of his family. Considering the region we are concerned with, Saladin bequeathed Egypt to his son al Aziz Uthman. After al Aziz's death, eventually Saladin's brother Al Adil took over as ruler of Egypt and he was succeeded as Egypt's ruler by his son al Kamil Mohammed I. The latter is important from our viewpoint as he reformed the coinage.

Ayyubid coins varied in style according to the different regions. In Egypt early Ayyubid dinars were of the 'bull's eye' style like those of the Fatimids **(58)**, although later ones reverted to a more traditional type. In Egypt the Ayyubids were short of gold: internal sources had diminished, the export trade had decreased and Egypt had to pay tribute to neighbours (to stop them invading) and Saladin had to send 'presents' –mainly gold coin – to Nur al Din, to whom, before he asserted his independence, Saladin was a vassal. During the late Ayyubid period, because it was scarce, 'gold became a commodity' (Balog 1964), coins varied in weight and so were weighed.

Silver took over and became the standard for the coinage.

Saladin was initially short of silver, so he had all the silver sashes removed from the prayer niches in the Cairo mosques. This had two purposes. It provided silver for coins and also removed the titles of the Fatimid Caliphs from the mosques. He was thus able to continue the issue of dirhems of low grade, the so called black dirhems, which were often very crude. He was indeed short of money, due to, among other things, the cost of his military activities during the second crusade. He frequently 'resorted to confiscation' (Rabie 1970), seizing the wealth of rich people. He also took the library of the Fatimids and auctioned it off. The gold and silver coins he minted in Egypt at first did not bear his name, but only that of his overlord Nur al Din Mahmud. After the latter's death he issued coins with his own name on one side and that of the Caliph al Mustadi on the other. Saladin did not mint copper coins in Egypt, 'for the simple reason that there were no adequate stocks of copper' there (Balog 1980). A few ayyubid fulus came into Egypt from Syria etc – brought in by traders and other travellers. During this period glass tokens continued to be used.

Eventually Saladin's nephew, al Kamil Mohammed I, who became ruler of Egypt and Sultan of the Empire, produced a copper coinage in Egypt, **(59)**, in 1225 A.D. (that is 622 A.H. i.e. Anno Herigae, - this dating system is explained in the Appendix). During the ayyubid period the script on coins changed. Since the Abbasids it had been kufic script, with emphasis on vertical lines and angles, as on items **(51), (54) & (54a)**, it then changed to naskhi, a more cursive form of writing, with less emphasis on verticals, see **(60), (62) & (63)**. Compare the first line of the kalima on **(54,a)** and **(60)**.

About this time an average workman's wage was about two to three dinars per month. A pound of bread cost about 0.0043 of a dinar, i.e. perhaps 1/12 dirhem, depending on the exchange rate. Wheat cost about 1 dinar for 100 Kgm. These figures should be taken with a pinch of salt. Wages varied between occupations and when pestilence or wars reduced populations, wages increased. Similarly food prices depended upon geographic variation and weather, wars and famines etc. For example earlier during the extreme famine in Mustansir's reign wheat was reported to cost the almost unbelievable price of 140 dinar per 100 Kgm, with bread similarly priced, although afterwards wheat dropped to about 1.79 dinars per 100 Kgm. (Ashtor 1976).

The Mamluks took over from their masters when the widow of the leading Ayyubid married a Mamluk and he was raised to the throne. The Mamluks ruled for over two and a half centuries, from 1250 A.D., and they consisted of two dynasties, the Bahri and Burji Mamluks. An early Bahri ruler, Baybars, had on silver and other coins his personal badge, a lion **(60), (60a).** He improved the fineness of the silver coins, issuing some of seventy per cent. The exchange rate was twenty Dirhems to a Dinar. The coins initially still exhibited a modified version of the Kalima **(60).** Mamluk coins were struck at several mints, principally Cairo and Alexandria, but also at others outside Egypt. Many bear the Cairo mintmark **(60), (66).** Baybars was followed by his sons, the second of whom, Salamish, **(62)** was young and ruled with a regent, Qalawoun, who quickly succeeded him **(63).** During the Bahri period succession was often inherited. A major family was that of Qalawoun, Among his descendants one of the greatest was al Nasir Mohammed **(64).** As noted earlier Mamluk coins often included the titles "Sultan, Malik" e.g. **(64).** Architecture is discussed below but we recall the first mosque in the citadel was built by al Nasir, he also patronised small arts, for example glass lamps, like the one on a modern coin **(127).** A distinctive feature of Mamluk copper coins is that many had designs such as animals, flowers, birds or wheels, stars and other geometric patterns **(61), (66),** which may have been heraldic signs of the various rulers. Most of these came from Mamluk mints outside Egypt. Some of these coins were initially underweight, but it was then decreed one fals should equal the weight of one silver dirhem **(61).** From the Cairo mint initially there were relatively few copper coins but later in the reign of Mansur Mohammed **(66)** there was an avalanche of copper (Balog 1964).

The Mamluks had inherited the Ayyubid practice of treating gold as a commodity. During this period gold was traded by weight in the form of stamped –ingots, sometimes called ingot-dinars (Album 2011), these coins had different irregular weights, from three grams to fifteen grams. In the late Bahri period Egypt experienced serious inflation which caused considerable distress to the population (Balog 1964) Much later a Burji Mamluk Faraj (c 810 A.H), trying to stabilise gold, devalued the dinar from 4.25 to 3.45 grams. The new coin, later taken over by Barsbay, often had inscriptions between 'cable' designs, and was called an Ashrafi, after one of Barsbay's titles **(67).** About this time the date on coins started appearing in numerals **(67),** previously it had been in words. It is worth recalling that the dinar had been based initially on the Byzantine gold coin which had followed on from the Roman solidus which was introduced by Constantine at 4.4 grams in about 330 A.D. So there had been a gold coin of a relatively stable weight, just over four grams., in the region for more than 1000 years. So Faraj's debasement was the first major gold currency devaluation. Initially in the long Mamluk period, dirhems, for example those of Baybars, were about 3 grams and there were also ½ dirhems of 1.5. grams. Later on, by the reign of Kait Bey, the dirhems were reduced to about 1.4 grams **(68)**. Kait Bey had a long reign and is well known for his buildings. However at the time the people suffered considerably due to the taxation needed for this building programme. Even later dirhems were reduced to one gram. In about 1500, in addition to the weight decrease, the percentage silver of dirhems was decreased.

Recent bank notes illustrating some Islamic architecture

Cairo is mainly a medieval city, not an ancient one. Some of the most notable buildings there are the mosques, some of which were mentioned earlier. Egypt has taken the opportunity of using its currency to display some of these both to its population and to the world. The mosques illustrate some of the developments in Islamic architecture, showing the different styles which occurred in different periods. Over the centuries, throughout the Islamic world, the tower, the minaret, of a mosque has been an important feature. Originally square, sometimes short, it became cylindrical, taller, often three tiered and more elaborate, so that at one stage the upper tier became like a small pavilion. Then eventually the minaret became very tall, slender and less elaborate.

Recent Egyptian currency notes show this development. The LE 5 note **(69a)** shows both the minaret and part of the fortified quadrangle of the ibn Tulun mosque. The al Azhar mosque of the Fatamids is seen both on the 50 piastre note **(69b)** and on a special coin issued recently to celebrate its 1000th anniversary **(120)**. Illustrating Mamluk architecture; the elaborate Kait Bey tomb is on the LE 1 **(69c)**, the Sultan Hasan mosque – one of the best examples of Islamic architecture - is on the LE 100 **(69d)**, the Kani Bey mosque is on the LE 200 **(140)**, and the Abu Hureba is on the LE 50 **(69e)**. On the LE 50 the top tier in the form of a pavilion is clearly seen. It is perhaps useful to note that the

Abu Hureba mosque is labelled as such on the LE 50 but on maps of Cairo it is often called the el Ishaqi mosque. El Ishaqi was the Master of Horse to Kait Bey. The Qalawoun mosque is on an old LE 10 note **(69f)**. Finally, as will be seen in the next section, the Mohammed Ali mosque, the crowning feature of the citadel, is an example of a mosque with tall slender minarets.

Several of these mosques can be seen on a short walk through a part of Cairo. This walk is described in the Appendix. Outside Cairo, a Mamluk mosque in Alexandria is seen on an old 25 piastre note **(70)**.

6

EGYPTIAN OTTOMAN COINS

The Ottoman Empire and its currency

For four centuries from 1517 A.D., Egypt was part of the Ottoman Empire and its coinage was influenced by, indeed tied to that of the Empire. So an outline of the ottoman currency is useful for an understanding of egyptian coins of the period.

The Ottoman Empire originated in Asia Minor, in the 1300s. The Ottomans were a turkish people, not arabs. In 1453, under Mohammed II, Constantinople and surrounding lands were conquered. Later other regions, the Levant, Egypt and other parts of North Africa were added to the Empire.

The ottoman currency initially consisted of small silver coins, akces **(71)**, of about one gram, and copper mangirs **(72)** of about three grams. Debasement of the silver coins was used to finance military campaigns and other activities. The silver content of the akce was reduced by thirty per cent during the reign of MohammedII up to the year 1481. The first gold coin, the sultani was issued about 1480. The Empire adopted the policy of using the gold coin, the sultani, for instance that of Sulaiman I **(73),** in all territories, but leaving the silver and copper coins already in use in the provinces practically as they were. There were further silver coin debasements, including a massive one in 1585 of fortyfour percent to finance costly wars with Iran. By then the akce was unusably small. So in the 1640s, they tried other silver coins, e.g. the para (equal to three akces) **(74)**, based on an existing egyptian coin. Later, at the time the Empire was at its zenith in 1690, they issued a new gold coin, the zeri mahbub, and some new large silver coins: the zolota, and importantly the kurus. The kurus initially weighed 26.0 grams, with sixty percent silver, i.e. containing 15.6 grams silver. It was to be worth 40 paras or 120 akces. The zolota, named after a large Polish coin used in international trade at the time, was worth three quarters of one kurus. The silver percentage of the kurus remained relatively stable, although the coin's total weight slowly reduced until about 1780 in Abdul Hamid I's reign **(75)** when it still contained about ten grams of silver. There was another large debasement in 1789 due to wars with Russia and Austria. The silver content of the kurus was reduced to 5.9 grams. In the reign of Mahmud II, 1808 – 1839, there was a series of large debasements, and one kurus was reduced from 5.9 to 0.53 grams silver, due to more wars with Russia, and the Greek wars of independence. In these years they tried to keep the kurus at a usable size, and so it was reduced to billon; usually less than fifty percent silver **(76)**. They also then issued billon five kurus coins. After this turbulence in the reign of Mahmud II they adopted in 1844 a new gold-silver standard with a new gold coin, the lira **(77)** equal to 100 new kuruses **(78)**, each of which consisted of one gram of silver. The new kurus was small and multiple coins, twenty kuruses etc., were issued for commercial purposes. There were also, for daily use, copper coins -paras **(79)**. These eventually became nickel, but otherwise this system remained stable until 1922.

For religious reasons, Islamic coins in general had no pictures or portraits. So aesthetic features could only occur in the script as calligraphy. An example of this on ottoman coins is the tughra, the Sultan's signature. Although initially reasonably decipherable, these for Sultan after Sultan became so stylised, they can be used for identification only with difficulty. Although a tughra occurs on many coins in this book, a reasonably clear one may be seen on the twenty para coin **(79)**. On ottoman coins the date consists of two parts: the year of the Sultan's accession, plus the regnal year. These together give an AH era date, which is described in the appendix. This is so on coins throughout the empire including Egypt. For example on a coin of Abdul Aziz **(88)** the accession date, ١٢٧٧ (1277), is at the bottom, and the regnal date, ٧ (7), is at the top. Together these give the coin's A.H date ١٢٨٤ (1284).

Egyptian coins within the ottoman coinage

By 1500 the Mamluk state was in a rundown condition with financial and other problems, as noted earlier. On the other hand the Ottoman Empire was prospering being led by a series of efficient Sultans engaged in expanding their domains. Under Selim the Ottomans encroached into Mamluk territory in North Syria where they were confronted by a Mamluk army which they defeated near Aleppo in 1516. Moving south, in 1517 they conquered the Mamluk territory of Egypt. There the Mamluks had in place a gold coin, the ashrafi, a reduced dirhem (of just over one gram silver) called a para (sometimes called a medin) and copper coins, fulus. The Ottomans replaced the ashrafi with the sultani and left the other coins in place, though they added the akce to the denominations, and changed their mintmarks from 'Cairo' to 'Misr' (Egypt). So early ottoman coins in Egypt were the sultani **(80),** the para **(81),** coppers – fulus, sometimes called mangirs, such as that of Ahmed I **(82),** and akces (which were similar to **71** except that being much later were lighter than that, about 0.5 gms). The para initially equalled about 1½ to 2 akces, but after the latter's debasements, the para by 1640 equalled three akces. At that time, Egypt had to pay Istanbul a yearly tribute of 500,000 gold coins. There were also then many foreign coins circulating in the country. C Vivian in her book 'The Western Desert of Egypt' notes the widespread occurrence of spanish dollars in ottoman times and, later, Maria Teresa talers in Egypt. Similarly, as implied above, there were large polish and other european coins circulating there. In the 1690s Cairo was told to issue new larger silver coins and the new gold coin the zeri mahbub, **(84)** but the Cairo officials were tardy and eventually issued the gold coin at a lower gold standard than advised which caused problems. In 1690 the para weighed 0.54 grams of seventy percent silver, i.e. roughly the same as the turkish para. Over the next century the egyptian para slowly reduced in weight but retained its fineness at over fifty percent **(83).** In the 1790s however, in line with the silver coins of Istanbul, it dropped in weight to 0.22 grams and in fineness to thirtyfive percent silver, i.e. it became billon **(85).** Then it dropped in quality even further up to the 1830s, when in Mahmud IIs reign the billon para was replaced with a copper one. Early in Mahmud's reign a billon five para coin was issued, which then also was replaced by a copper five para coin **(87).** Because they had had a relatively usable silver coin, the para, Cairo was slow in following the instructions to issue coins like the larger Istanbul silver coins, only producing them in 1769, calling the main one a guersh (equal to the kurus). In line with Istanbul's debasements in the next couple of decades, the guersh declined in silver content and by the early 1800s was reduced to billon, like the kurus. This reduction occurred in several stages, with increasingly poor billon at each stage **(86a & 86b).** During this period Egypt was becoming more independent politically, though still nominally acknowledging the Sultans in Istanbul and continuing to issue coins in their names. In 1805 the Sultan appointed Mohammed Ali as Pasha or governor. Later Mohammed Ali consolidated his position, the Sultan recognised him as hereditary ruler of Egypt. In 1834, as part of Mohammed Ali's reforms, Egypt adopted a new gold and silver currency standard. New gold coins, pounds, were issued, such as that of Abdul Aziz **(88),** equal to 100 new guersh **(89)** (sometimes called piastres, see the footnote at the end of this section) each weighing 1.25 grams (actually containing just over 1 gram silver, being 0.833 fine). While the guersh was the basic unit, it was small and for everyday transactions there were larger coins of ten and twenty guersh **(90)**. Also for use as change, there were smaller denominations in copper of 40, 20 and 10 para **(91)**, with 40 para equal to one guersh. It may be noted that consequently there were the two coins; a small silver guersh and a large copper 40 paras, which were equal in value and circulating at the same time. Some of the copper coins were later issued as bronze.

During the nineteenth century, many nations, following the lead of the United States and France, adopted a decimal currency. In the reign of Abdul Hamid II, Egypt stopped issuing paras and instead minted fractions (1/10th and multiples thereof) **(92)** of a guersh in cupronickel, and later, as even smaller change, 1/40 and 1/20 guersh coins in bronze **(96)**. Also, at about the turn of the century, the guersh was changed from a silver coin, which it was early in his reign, cf. **(93a)**, to a slightly larger cupronickel one **(93b)**. Larger denominations **(94)** remained silver.

All these coins continued to bear the Istanbul Sultans' names and the Tughra up to the first World War. Also in this period E.W. Lane (2003) mentioned that "the coins of Constantinople are current in Egypt: but scarce".

Some general points about currency in the Ottoman period

Early in the period, about 1525, the daily wage was about five akces and a loaf of bread cost one akce – about 0.7 grms silver. After the nineteenth century monetary reforms, the daily wage in Istanbul was about six kuruses and a loaf cost one kurus. As Pamek (2000) states "it is remarkable that even though nominal prices increased by about 300 times, prices expressed in grams of silver stayed within the narrow range, ….mostly between 0.7 and 1.5 during these four and a half centuries". In the late 1830s, wheat cost about six piastres per bushel and as the rural agricultural wage in Egypt was up to 80 paras per day, i.e. at most two piastres per day, a bushel of wheat could cost about three days' wages.

Concerning the everyday uses of coins by the population, sometimes coins have occasionally been used as ornaments - as jewellery. This usage peaked in the late nineteenth century, - recall british Victorian enamelled coin brooches etc., some of which still survive. Some egyptian coins were used in this way as necklaces, cuff-links **(93a)** etc. or even, among bedouin women, as complete veils. Some of this jewellery exhibited the dual allegiance felt by some people. The brooch illustrated **(104)** includes a turkish coin symbolizing the Empire and egyptian coins reflecting the country. Similarly ottoman coins like those of many nations were sometimes put to other non-monetary uses, e.g. some were made into spoons etc.

Some of the later nineteenth century and early twentieth century Egyptian coins were minted outside Egypt, for example many bear the H (Heaton) mintmark, as on the Mohhammed V coin **(95)**. Others bear for example KN **(97),** for the Kings Norton mint, or other initials for other european mints. Some Hussain Kamil coins were designed by Harvey Rowntree (Sweeny 1981). Some bear the initials HR **(102a)**. Some coins from Berlin have a W for the engraver rather than an initial for the city. Many of these coins with mintmarks etc. are still available on stalls in the Khan el Khalili, the big bazaar in Cairo. Turning briefly to a different topic, the Suez Canal was built in the 1860s by the French. For their egyptian employees the contractors issued token coins, now rare. Generally in Egypt in the early ottoman period there was a lack of cultural vitality; it vegetated as a backwater of the Empire. In the time of Mohammed Ali however, when Egypt was semi-independent of Constantinople, it revived and a major example of ottoman architecture, his mosque, was built in the Citadel at Cairo, as seen on current coins **(124)** and the LE 20 note **(98)**. Also at that time there was to an extent a harking back to earlier art, and the al Rifai mosque, seen on the two LE 10 notes **(99)** and **(100),** was built in a neo-mamluk style. There are two versions of the LE 10 note in circulation, one shows the exterior of the mosque, the other the interior. From this viewpoint the depiction of this mosque on the LE 10 is unique. The differentiation, noted in the preface, of the Egyptian state historically, into independent and not independent, is reflected in its architecture over the millennia. When Egypt was independent, e.g. under the Arabs, major buildings were erected, when it was not, e.g. under the Romans, few or no major buildings were erected.

Footnote: The name piastre came from the term piastra d'argento (plate of silver) which was a colloquial term for spanish coins such as Pieces of Eight in the early 1600s. It was then used widely in Europe and elsewhere for many silver coins similar to or derived from the spanish ones. It was used for example in Italy, Lebanon, Morocco, Cyprus, Tunisia, Turkey, Syria, Egypt and even South Vietnam. Although initially used for dollar sized coins it was later applied to smaller silver coins. In some countries piastre is/was an official denomination in the coinage, for example in Lebanon. Elsewhere it was used by people for coins which officially had other titles, as in nineteenth century Egypt, where a guersh was colloquially called a piastre. Later, during World War I and just afterwards, Egypt issued coins **(102)** labelled piastre in english and guersh in arabic, on the same coin.

THE TWENTIETH CENTURY

The first half century

In the first decade or so of the twentieth century in Egypt the ottoman coinage of Abdul Hamid continued and was followed by that of Mohammed V. In the latter's reign the guersh, which had reverted briefly to being a silver coin, was changed again to a slightly larger cupronickel coin.

Egypt saw many political changes in the twentieth century. Initially it was nominally subject to the Ottoman Sultanate in Istanbul. In 1914 at the start of World War I, Turkey became an ally of the Germans, while Egypt joined Britain and its allies. In that year the British ended the Turkish rule of Egypt by making it a British protectorate. Egypt became a Sultanate itself. The Egyptian ruler Hussain Kamil was raised by the British to the rank of Sultan, i.e. equal to the turkish ruler. So for some years there was the Istanbul ottoman Sultan and a local egyptian Sultan, whose coins declared his status **(101)** and recorded that they were issued in the Egyptian Sultanate, *Sultanat es Misriyat* **(102)**, (for the detail of the arabic of this and other egyptian titles in this section, see the Appendix). Fuad **(103)**, who became Sultan after Hussain Kamil, had similar expressions on his coins.

During the war there were radical alterations to the monetary system, and a european/british influence could be seen. The following half dozen or so changes occurred.

First, as just noted, the coins were issued in the name of the Egyptian Sultanate.

Second, the coinage denomination structure changed. Instead of involving a piastre (guersh) and fractions thereof, it included a piastre which consisted of ten milliemes **(97)**, with 100 piastres making an egyptian pound, i.e. with 1000 milliemes to the pound. 1 millieme coins were issued at this period and later. Also, the coinage metal changed. From 1916 the piastre coin ceased to be silver being replaced with a ten millieme coin in cupronickel, though the two piastre remained as silver, as in the brooch noted earlier. It is noteworthy that that brooch was made in (or after) the war in which Turkey was the enemy yet the brooch still indicates an affiliation to Turkey.

Third, as noted in the footnote to the previous section, the coin's title, i.e. its denomination, was, on the same coin, in two languages: "Piastre" in roman letters and "Guersh" in arabic script.

Fourth, in line with the last point, the denomination number was similarly expressed twice: both as a roman numeral and as an arabic numeral.

Fifth, not only did the denomination number occur as a roman numeral, on lower value coins it occurred as english words, "ten" **(97)** and "five". This was the first time English words occurred on Egyptian coins, - assuming "Piastre" is seen as a european word, rather than specifically english.

Sixth, with regard to the dates, the coins exhibit two different approaches to recording dates. The obverse of the coins in line with ottoman procedures presents the accession date of the ruler, ١٣٣٣ (1333) **(101)**. The reverse, on many coins presents, as on western coins, the actual date. This occurs twice, both as an "A.D." date in roman numerals, 1917, and as an "A.H." date in arabic numerals, ١٣٣٥ (1335) **(102)**.

After the war the Ottoman Caliphate and Sultanate and the title of Sultan were abolished, as was the Egyptian Sultanate. Fuad was made King in 1922 and coins **(105)** were issued with his portrait and new title, King of Egypt *Malik Misr.* It is to be noted that this involved a radical change on Islamic coins which previously had not depicted portraits for religious reasons. It is also to be noted that on his early coins before 1922 Fuad was entitled 'Sultan' and on his later ones 'King'. During his reign as king, on his first coinage Fuad faced the right and on his second coinage he faced left.

Fuad was followed as king by his son Farouk **(106a, 106b & 108)** who ruled until he was deposed by a revolution in 1952. During Farouk's reign commemorative gold coins were issued for his wedding in 1938 **(107)**.

During the first half of the century, some coins were produced with unusual shapes rather than the traditional shape of a solid circular disc. Initially some circular coins had a hole in the middle. **(97).** Then also there were hexagonal coins **(106a).**

Later Farouk issued some bronze coins with scallop edges **(106b).** These coin shapes did not persist, although in the 1990s coins with a hole in the middle occurred again.

Republican Egypt

Egypt became a republic in 1953. Coins proclaiming this new status, the Republic of Egypt, *El Jomhuryat Misr*, were issued and a common obverse design of this period was the sphinx **(109)**. The most impressive coins were a gold LE 1, **(110)** an LE ½ and LE 5, which all show Rameses II riding a chariot. This design has also been used on later gold coins. After the revolution, a lot of public utilities and large factories and the Suez Canal **(111)** were nationalised and there were wide ranging land ownership reforms: former royal estates were taken over and major parts of large private estates were purchased compulsorily and this land was redistributed to smallholders.

The National Assembly was inaugurated **(113)**. The British were evacuated **(112)**. Thus in this period the design of coins included a propaganda function.

For a brief while from 1958 to 1971 Egypt became part of the United Arab Republic (the UAR) along with Syria and the Yemen. However this did not last long, Syria having withdrawn in 1961. During the brief period, 1958 -61, a common coin design was a falcon with a coat of arms on its breast **(115a & b).**This design was also used on syrian coins of the period. There was also a coin **(114)** celebrating the Agricultural and Industrial Fair of 1958. At the end of the period, a Nasser commemorative coin was issued **(116)**. After being part of the United Arab Republic, Egypt became the Arab Republic of Egypt. On everyday coins from 1953, items representative of Egypt were exhibited: the sphinx, pyramids **(117)** and later (surprisingly as Egypt had discarded the ottoman connection and sultans) a tughra.

In the second half of the century, the republic experienced many major events for which commemorative coins were issued. The Suez Canal was nationalised, invaded, blocked and then reopened **(122).**

The Nile was diverted **(118)**. The Aswan dam was built with its power station **(119)**. Egypt was at war with Israel **(121),** with which it later signed a peace treaty. Also as noted earlier, the Al Azhar mosque celebrated its 1000 years anniversary **(120)**. Some of the coins illustrate geographic features, e.g. Port Said **(111 & 122)** and the Aswan dam. During the monarchy the Head of State was portrayed continually on the coins. However during the republic, the Head of State appeared only infrequently on the coins. Nasser was depicted on coins of 1970, the year of his death, and Sadat appeared on coins of 1980 celebrating the peace treaty with Israel **(123)**.

Up to the UAR, mid-value coins, e.g. twenty piastres **(109)** were issued in silver. Later in the Arab Republic of Egypt they became cupro-nickel **(124)**. Also during this period in the second half of the century literally dozens of coins were issued which illustrated aspects of Egyptian life: the parliament, the National Bank, international women's year, Cairo trade fair, the applied professions **(125)**, national education, the Cairo subway, etc. Probably these coins were issued as much for collectors as for use in the circulating currency. Rarely do we find women depicted on coins, but Umm Kalsoum, the famous egyptian singer, is seen on coins of 1976 **(128)**. In addition, illustrating another art, a coin of the period exhibits a mamluk enamelled glass lamp from a mosque **(127)**. Also as noted earlier, the picture of Rameses II in a chariot was repeated on a gold coin in the 1980s **(126)**.

During the twentieth century Egypt, like the UK and other countries, moved from a routine gold pound coin to bank notes of which it has issued a variety. After a decree in 1898, a short range of notes was issued in 1899. However Egypt has retained occasional gold bullion and ceremonial pound coins, like those noted above **(107)**, **(110)**.

Recent banknotes have illustrated interesting features of Egypt's past. Each of these recent notes has typically on one side illustrated a mosque – some of these were noted earlier - and on the other side some aspect of ancient Egypt; people or buildings, and some of these also were noted earlier. Khafre, builder of the second pyramid, is shown on the LE 10 note **(129),** and an important feature of the karnak temple, i.e. pillars representing north and south Egypt, is seen on an old LE 10 note **(130)**. The mighty Pharaoh Rameses II, whose temple at Abu Simbel is on the LE 1 note **(131)**, is shown on the 50 Piastre note **(132)** along with his name in hieroglyphics, (for the details of which see the Appendix).

The best known Pharaoh Tutankhamun was portrayed on early bank notes but more recently his portrait has become the watermark in bank notes. As noted earlier, it is unusual for the currency to depict women, but Nefertiti, wife of Akhnaton, is seen on the 5 piastre note **(133),** her portrait bust being now in a Berlin museum. The LE 200 **(134)** depicts a scribe and a cartouche containing his name, which is detailed in the appendix.

Among recent coins there is another depicting the Al Azhar mosque **(135).** In the last decades of the twentieth century Egypt, in addition to small value coins, has used low denomination notes which soon became grubby and were not very durable. However around the millenium it has issued new LE 1 **(136),** 50 **(138)** and 25 piastre **(139)** coins. On the pound coin, the value occurs twice on the reverse, in english as 'One pound' and in arabic as 'One ginee' **(137).** An additional illustration for 'A walk in Islamic Cairo' in the Appendix- to be seen with items 69a to 69e – is **(140)** LE200 Kani Bey.

1

2

3

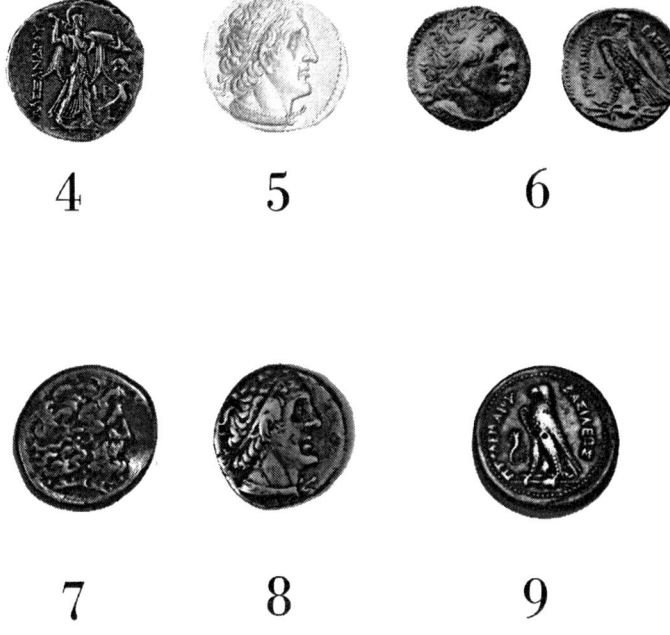

4   5   6

7   8   9

11   12

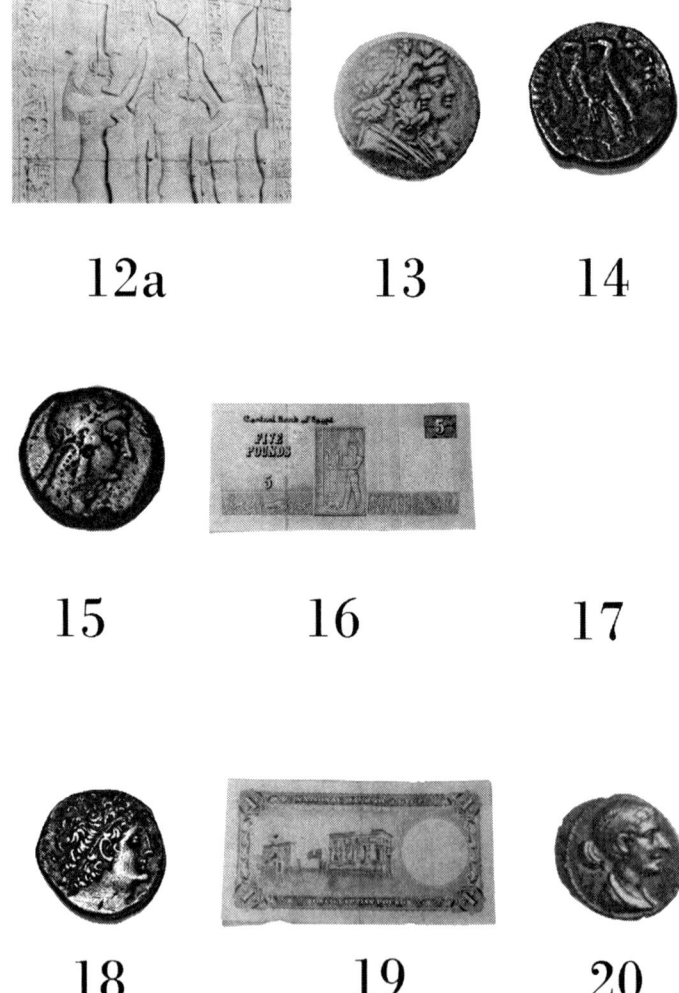

12a   13   14

15   16   17

18   19   20

21   22   23

24   25   26

27   28   29

30   31   32

33   34   35

36   37   38

39

40

41

42

43

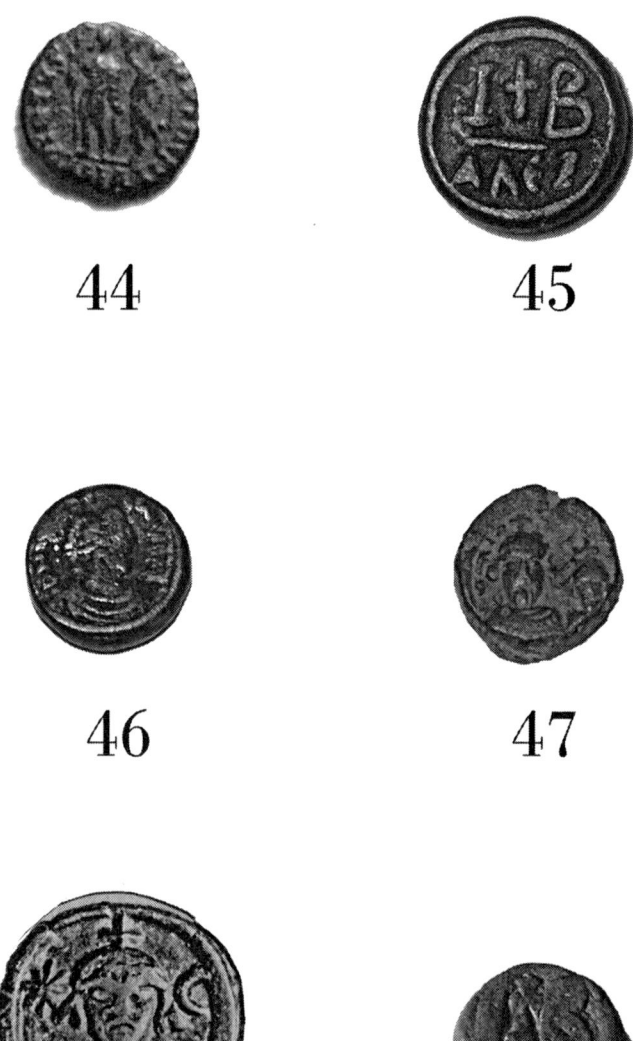

44

45

46

47

48

49

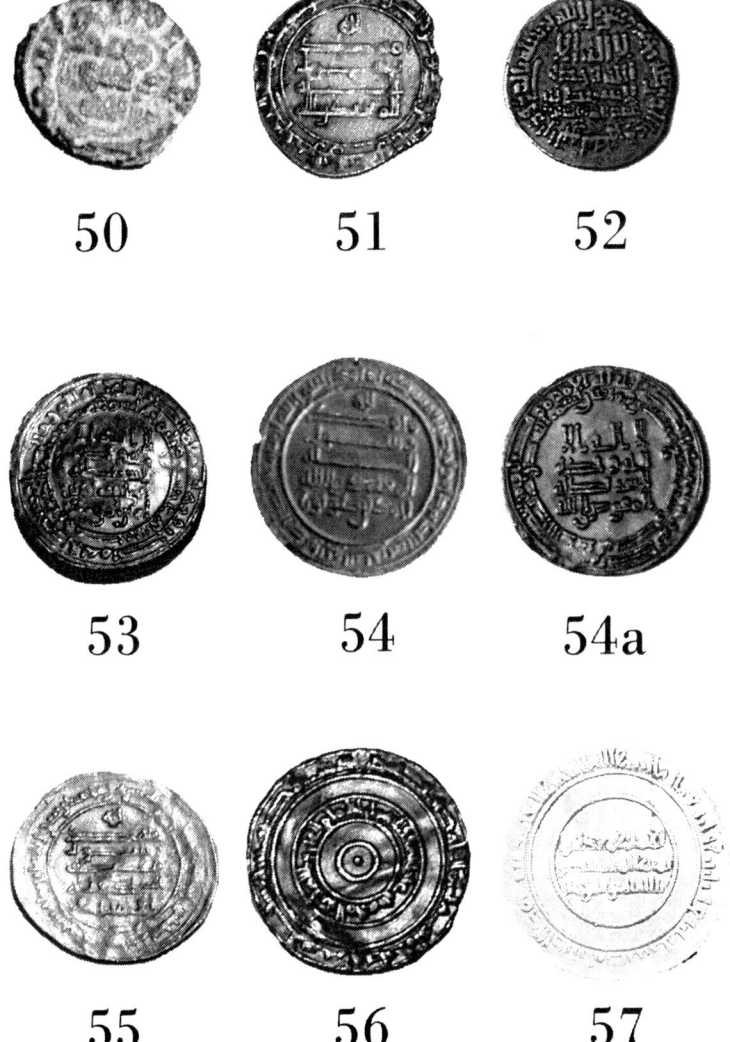

50   51   52

53   54   54a

55   56   57

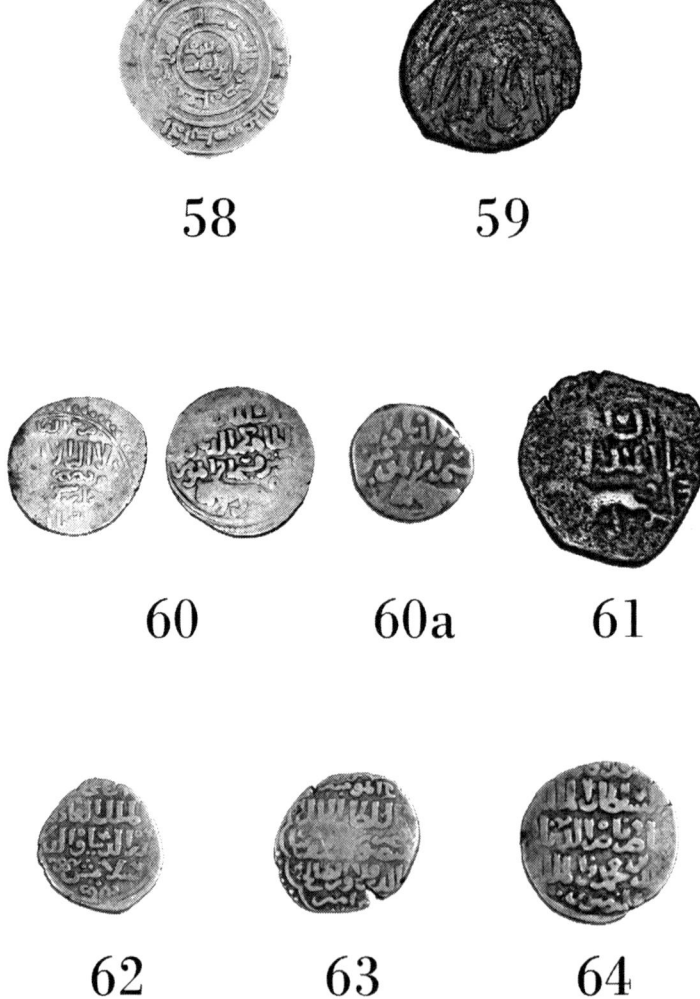

58   59

60   60a   61

62   63   64

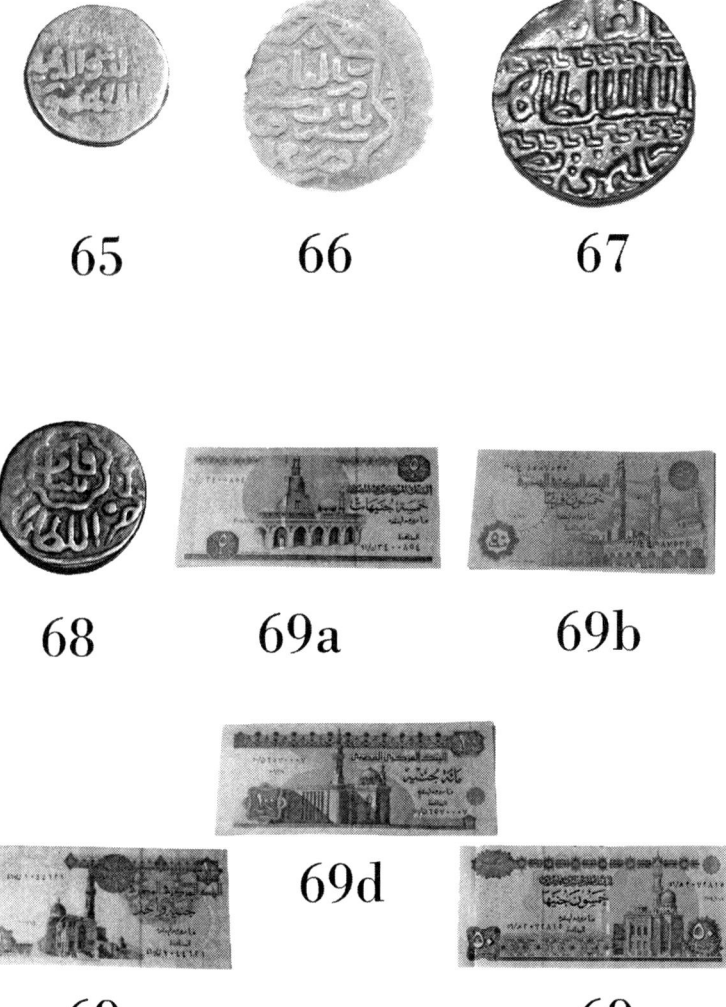

65   66   67

68   69a   69b

69d

69c   69e

70

71   72   73

74   75   76

77   78   79

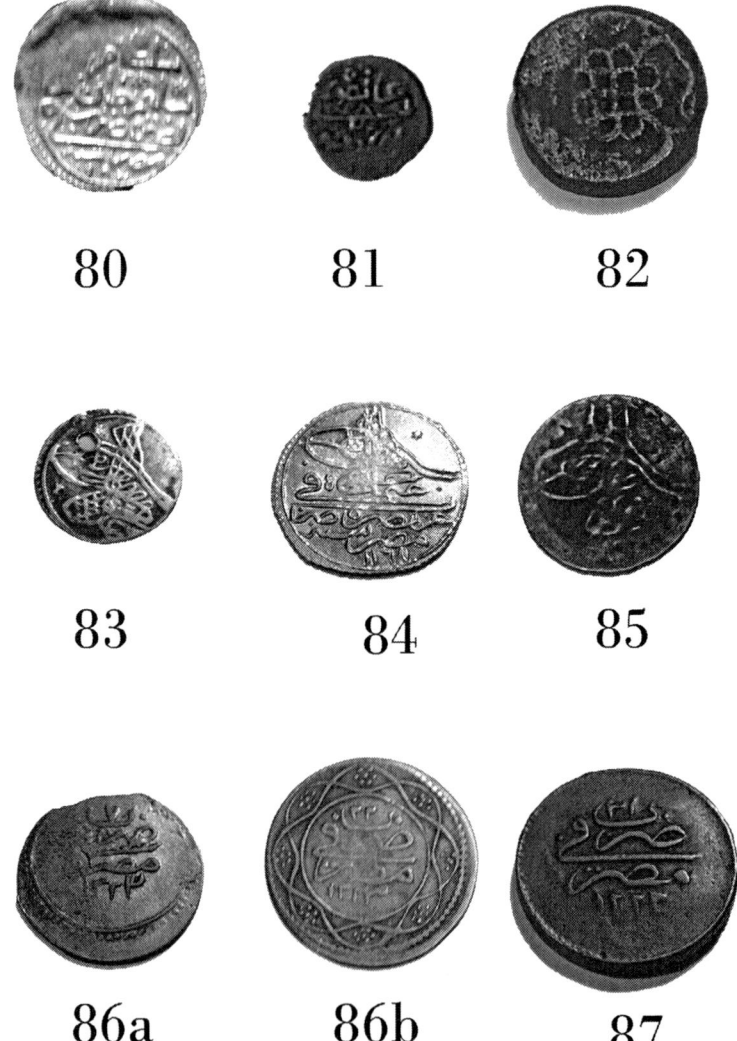

80   81   82

83   84   85

86a   86b   87

88   89   90

91   92   93a

93b   94   95

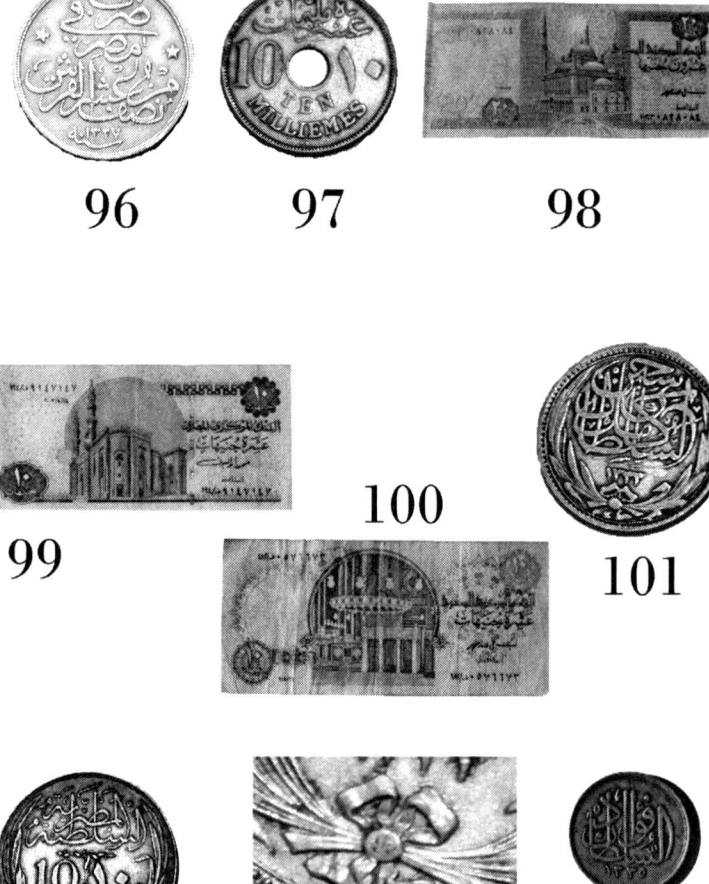

96   97   98

99   100   101

102   102a   103

104

105

106

106a

107

108

109

110

111

112   113   114

115a   115b   116

117   118   119

120 121 122 123

124 125 126 127

128 129 130

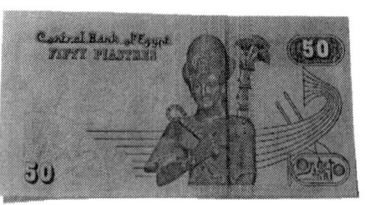

131

132

133

134

135

136

137

138

139

140

Key to currency illustrations and Timeline

<u>Abbreviations</u>: Au, Gold. Ar, Silver. Ae, Bronze. Bi, Billon. Brs, Brass. C-N, Cupro nickel. C, Copper. Br, Bronze, modern. A-B, Aluminium-Bronze O, Obverse, R, Reverse. Gr, Grams. mm, millimetre. mmk, Mint mark P, Piastre. LE, Egyptian pound, and Tetra. for Tetradrachm. and also Hd for head, with L or Rt for head facing to the left or right

NB.

The illustrations do not show the actual size of the coins.

The actual sizes are as indicated in this list. The measurements of a coin in this list are those of the actual coin illustrated. They do not indicate the standard or official size of the coin type. Indeed an illustrated coin might be slightly less in weight etc than the standard weight due to wear during daily use etc.

<u>Illustrated face of coin</u>   <u>Other face of coin</u>

Figures in the left-hand column are dates which, with the list, provide a basic timeline.

B.C.

		Illustrated face of coin	Other face of coin
	1.	Athenian owl, copy, 20 mm	Head of Athena
360	2.	Nectanebo Au Stater. 8.53 gr. 16 mm.	A horse
332	3.	Alexander, Ar Tetra. Zeus, Mmk Memphis. 28 mm, 15.6 gr	Head of Alexander
305	4.	Ptolemy I, Ar Tetra. Alkidemos 28 mm14 gr	Head of Alexander
	5.	Ptolemy I Au Stater. 7 gr. 18 mm.	Alexander in a chariot pulled by elephants
	6.	Ptolemy I Ar Tetra, both faces	A common Ptolemaic

		14.2 gr. 24 mm,	reverse is an Eagle on a thunderbolt & the legend ΠΤΟΛΕΜΑΪΟΥ ΒΑΣΙΛΕΩΣ (King Ptolemy).In this list 'Eagle & legend' stands for this.
	7.	Ptolemy III Ae 37, 18.7 gr. Head of Zeus	R. Eagle & legend
	8.	Ptolemy II Ar Tetra, head of Ptolemy I	Eagle & legend,
		25 mm, 14.1 gr	mmk Σ I
246	9.	Ptolemy III Ae 42, 74 gr	Head of Zeus Ammon
	10.	Arsinoe II Au Octodrachm on a 100mil 1977 stamp of Cyprus.	
	11.	LE 50 bank note, Edfu temple	For other face see 69e
	12.	LE 20 bank note	For other face see 98
	12a.	Picture of Ptolemy III in Edfu temple	
	13.	Ptolemy IV, Serapis & Isis, Ar Tetra, 24mm, R Eagle & legend	
180	14.	Ptolemy VI, Ae 29, 22.4 gr. 2 eagles	O. Head of Zeus Ammon
	15.	Cleopatra I as Isis Ae 26. 16 gr	R. Eagle & legend
	16	LE 5 banknote	For other face see 69a
	17.	Ptolemy VIII ArTetra on a 60 mil 1977 stamp of Cyprus	
106	18.	Ptolemy X Ar Tetra, 22 mm. 14.1gr	Eagle & legend, mmk ΠΑ
	19.	Old LE 1 banknote, Philae	
51	20.	Cleopatra VII Ae 26,	R. Eagle & this legend ΚΛΕΟΠΑΤΡΑΣ ΒΑΣΙΛΙΣΣΗΣ (Queen Cleopatra)
		80 Ae. drachmai = 1 obol	

Unless stated otherwise, the items from 21 to 38 are billon tetradrachms. Most of the illustrations are of coin reverses. The other face, if not stated otherwise, is a profile bust of the named emperor, facing right (Rt) or left (L). The coins to no.38 show the regnal year in greek numerals, i.e. greek letters, preface by L, which stands for 'year', e.g. 'LA'. In this list these are translated into english, i.e. 'LA' is 'Year 1' etc.

N.B. Items between 26 and 40 were issued between 117 & 295 A.D, but their order in this list is determined by the order of topics in the text, not their actual dates within this period.

A.D.

	21	Augustus, Ae26 (obel) 17.3gm	Caesar Autocrat
20	22	Tiberius, head of, 24 mm, 10.8 gr. year 7	Head of Augustus
65	23	Nero, ship, 24 mm, 13.5 gr	Nero, L. year 1
	24	Nero, Poseidon, 24 mm, 13.1 gr	Nero, L. year 1
	25	Vespasian, year 1, 24 mm. 12.4 g	Eirene (Pax)
117	26	Hadrian, 'Alexandria' greets Hadrian 24 mm. 8.3 gr	Hadrian, year 15
	27	Antinoos, Chalkon, 9mm	man & Caduceus
	28	Nero, Apollo, year 13, 25 mm. 13.5 gr	Nero, Rt
	29	Trajan, Nilus, year 18, 24 mm. 13.3 gr	Trajan, Rt
138	30	Antoninus Pius, Serapis, year 7, 23 mm. 12.4 gr	Antoninus Pius Rt
	31	Nero, 'Alexandria', year 12, 24 mm. 11.6 gr	Nero Rt
	32	Hadrian, Brs. Medalion, Aesculapius, 60mm. 81.gr.	Hadrian L
	33	Antoninus Pius, Ae 32, Isis before the Pharos, 23.2 gr. DODEKATOY (In Greek), i.e. year 12	Antoninus Pius Rt
	34	Antoninus Pius, Ae 32, Zodiac: Venus in Taurus 17.2 gr. Year 8	Antoninus Pius Rt
	35	Marcus Aurelius, Ae 32, the Caesarium?, 20.5 gr	Marcus Aurelius

67

288	36	Maximianus, year 2, 20 mm, 8.1 gr	Eagle
	37	Nome coin: Ae. 5.6g.,18mm.Arsinoe II	Hadrian
	38	M Aurelius (chipped) 24mm. 7.8 gr	Hd. Zeus Ammon
		Commodus 24 mm. 11.6 gr	Zeus enthroned.
	39	Maximianus, Ae. antoninianus, mmk ALE 24mm. 3.1 gr	Hd of Maximianus
295	40	Diocletian Ar Follis. 25mm.10.2gr. Mmk ALE	Diocletian Rt
	41	Constantine, Ae 4, mmk ALE. 14 mm 1.2 gr	Hd of Constantin
	42	Constans with labarum, Ae. a reduced centenionalis, 17 mm. 2.7 gr	Hd of Constans
	43	Valens, Au. Solidus. 20 mm. 4.1 gr	Hd of Valens
400	44	Arcadius Ae. 15mm. 2.5 grm. mmk ALE	Bust of Arcadius
527	45	Justinian, Ae. 12 nummi, i.e. with I.B. 14 mm. 3.1 gr. Mmk ALEZ, in greek	Hd of Justinian
	46	Justinian, Ae. 12 nummi, profile head, 16 mm. 5.2 gr.	I.B & plain cross
613	47	Heraclius and Heraclius Constantine, Ae. 12 nummi. 15 mm. 4.7 gr	I.B & cross&steps
620	48	Khusru II, Ae.12 nummi, 5.1 gr	I.B & cross&globe
	49	a thick 12 nummi coin, 16 mm. 9.2 gr	

ARABIAN

	50	Ae fals 20 mm, 6.3 gr. Kalima	2nd part of Kalima
740		name of finance minister	

Abbasid

	51	Ar Dirhem 25 mm, 2.6 gr 2nd part of Kalima	Kalima
810	52	Al Mamun Au Dinar, 17 mm, 4.1 gr	2nd part of Kalima
		Kalima	
	53	Muqtadir Au Dinar 25 mm, 4.3 gr	

Tulunid

| | 54 | ibn Tulun Au Dinar, Rev. | Obverse similar
to |
| 868 | | 23 mm, 4.14 gr | that of 54a On
this reverse, after
the 3 lines of the
2nd part of the
Kalima, are 2
further lines; the
first is the name
of the caliph, al
Mu'tamid, the
other is the name
of the issuer,
Ahmad ibn Tulun |

54a Khumarawayh ibn Tulun Au Dinar
Obv

Rev similar to 54 mutatis mutandis On this obverse there are 2 circles of legend. The inner circle legend (starting with Bismillah) gives the coin's value, date of issue and mint location, here Misr (Egypt). It is noteworthy that the date is presented in words not numerals.

Ikhshidid

55 Abu Baker Au Dinar 23mm, 3.1 grm   Kalima

Fatimid

975 56 Al Aziz Au Dinar 23mm, 4.1 gr

1035 57 Al Mustansir Au Dinar 22mm. 4.3 gr   Kalima

Ayyubid

1170 58 Saladin Au Dinar 20mm 4.4 gr
Saladin's name

1220 59 Al Kamil Mohammed I. Ae fals 25 mm, 3.6 gr

Mamluk

1260 60 Baybars Ar Dirhem, 20 mm,   Baybars 21mm, 2.9g

mmk 'Cairo' above the Kalima   lion below
Baybars' name

(These 2 faces, although typical of this coin type, are actually of different coins)

	60a	Baybars Ar ½ Dirhem 15mm 1.4gr	
	61	Baybars Ae fals 21 mm, 2.6 g	
	62	Salmish Ar D'hem 21mm 2.6gm	Cairo m
	63	Kala'oun Ar D'hem 23mm 2.8gr	Kalima
1300,	64	al Nasir Mohammed Ar. D'hem 22mm 2.9 gr. Ruler's name	Kalima
	65	al Mansur Mohammed Ar D'hem 20mm,3.3gr	
	66	Al Mansur Mohammed Ae fals. 23mm 4.1 gr. Cairo mmk	Ruler's name
67		Al Zahir Khushqadam Au Dinar 15 mm, 3.4 gr	
1461		Mmk 'Cairo' above Al Zahir	
	68	Kait Bey Ar Dirhem 15 mm,1.5 gr	

His name is in the inner circle

Recent bank notes illustrating mosque architecture etc. from the above periods.

	69a	LE 5 note, ibn Tulun	for other face see 16
	69b	50 Piastre note, al Azhar	for other face see 132
	69c	LE 1, Kait Bey tomb	for other face see131
	69d	LE 100, Sultan Hasan	a sphinx
	69e	LE 50, Abu Hureba	for other face see 11
	69f	old LE10, Kala'oun	A Sakiyah
	70	old 25 piastre, Mosque in Alexandria	

Some of these notes provide 'signposts' for "A walk in islamic Cairo" (which is in the Appendix).

In the following, up to item 97, dates are in the A.H. system. On the coins they are in arabic numerals, and the dates given here are the accession dates

Ottoman Empire coins

1512 71 899 Ar Akce 0.8 gr. 19 mm.
72 Sulaiman II Ae Mangir 1099   Tughra
1.3 gr. 19 mm.
73 Sulaiman I Au Sultani 20 mm,
3.5 gr
mmk. Amasya
74 Ahmed III Ar Para 1115.   Tughra
0.65gr. 15mm.
mmk Constantinople
75 Abdul Hamid I Ar Kurus 1187   Inscription
40mm. 19.3g
76 Mahmud II Bi Kurus 1223.
27mm. 2.8gr
77 Mohammed V Au Lira 22 mm,
7.2 gr
78 Murad V Ar new Kurus
1293.14mm. 1.2gr. Tughra
79 Abdul Aziz C 20 Para 1277
For another imperial ottoman coin of Mohammed V see the brooch **(104)** below

Ottoman Egyptian coins
1574 80 Murad III Au Sultani 22mm
3.5gr
1623 81 Murad IV Ar Para 15 mm, 0.8
gr
82 Ahmed I Ae Mangir 18 mm,   Misr
10.4 gr
83 Mahmud I Ar Para 0.4gr 15mm   1143
84 Osman III Au Zeri Mahbub
2.7gr, 21mm

1789	85	Selim III, Bi Para 15 mm, 0.2 gr	1203
	86a	Mahmud II Bi Guersh 5.3gm 30mm	Tughra
1808	86b	Mahmud II Bi Guersh 1223, 26 mm, 2.4 gr	Tughra
	87	Mahmud II C 5 Para 22 mm, 6.9 gr	Tughra
1861	88	Abdul Aziz Au LEl 1277 21mm, 8.6 gr	Tughra
	89	Abdul Aziz Ar new Guersh 1277 17 mm, 1.2 gr	Date & misr
	90	Abdul Aziz Ar 10 new Guersh 1277 28 mm, 12.4 gr	Date & misr
	91	Abdul Aziz Br 40, 20 & 10 Para 1277	
	92	Abdul Hamid II C-N, 3 fractional Guersh	Tughra
	93a	Cuff-links, a silver Guersh, 1293	
	93b	Abdul Hamid II, a C-N Guersh 1293 22 mm, 5.4 gr	Tughra
	94	Murad V Ar 10 guersh 14gr, 32mm	W,the engraver's initial
1909	95	Mohammed V Ar 20 Guersh, 1327 40 mm, 28.1 gr Tughra, with 'H' mmk	Misr with date
	96	Mohammed V Br. 1/20 Guersh 20mm. 3.3 gr.	Tughra & H mmk
	97	Husain Kamil, CN, 10 Milliemes	Accession date1333
		'KN' mmk coin, 26 mm, 5.8 gr	See 104

Bank notes illustrating mosques of this period

98	LE 20 Mohammed Ali mosque	for the other face see12
99	LE 10 Rifai mosque exterior	for the other face see 129
100	LE 10 Rifai mosque interior	ditto
101	Husain Kamil Ag 10 Piastre 32 mm, 14 gr	see 102 for reverse
102	Husain Kamil Ag sultanate. 1917	see101 for obverse

For a 2 Piastre coin of this series see the brooch (94).

102a	Photo of HR on Husain Kamil coin	
103	Fuad, Sultan, Ag 20 Piastre. 40mm.27.8g	value & date
104	Brooch, with Egyptian,2 piastres, and Imperial Ottoman 2 kurus coins	
1922	105	Fuad, as king, Ag 10 Piastre, 32mm, 14 gr
		Fuad the First, King of Egypt
	106a	Farouk, Ag 2 Piastre, 18 mm, 2.8 gr
	106b	Farouk, Br 10milliemes 6.1gr 25mm	Value
	107	Farouk, Au 20 Piastre, 14 mm, 1.7 gr.	Wedding, 1938
	108	Farouk Ar 10 Piastre 33mm. 14gr	value
	1953	Republican coins etc
	109	5 Milliemes A-B, Sphinx	value
	109	Title of the Republic, Ag 20 Piastre. 32 mm, 13.8 gr	Sphinx & date 1956
	110	gold pound Rameses II, 8.5gr 24mm	
	111	Nationalisation of Suez Canal Ar 25 P. 35mm. 17.5 gr.	value &1956

	112	Evacuation of British Ar. 50 P. 40mm 28gr	value, 195
	113	National Congress Ar 25 P 35mm. 17.5gr	value, 1957
	114	Agriculture & Industry A-B 20 Milliemes 24 mm, 5.8 gr	1958, value
	115a	1 millieme Br 16mm 1.9gr	
	115b	Falcon C-N 10 Piastre, 26 mm,5.8gr.	United Arab Repub',1967
1970	116	Nasser, Ar 50 Piastre, 32 mm,12.6gr.	Value & date 1970
	117	Pyramids A-B 5 Piastre 22mm	Tughra & value
	118	Diversion of the Nile, Ar 50 Piastre 40 mm, 19.9 gr	Value
	119	Aswan dam, Ar. 1 Pound, 40 mm, 25.2 gr	value, 1968
	120	Al Azhar mosque Ag 1 Pound 40 mm, 25.2 gr	value, 1970-72

63

	121	War LE1 Ar, 35mm 15.3gr	Val
	122	Suez Canal reopening, Ar 1 Pound 35 mm, 15.1 gr Port Said	1976
1980	123	Sadat, peace treaty, C-N 10 Piastre,26mm 6gr	value
	124	Mohammed Ali mosque C-N 20 Piastre,26mm,6gr	value, 198
	125	Professions Ar 1 Pound, 35 mm, 15.3 gr	Value & date 1980
	126	Rameses II Au. 32mm	Value LE100, 1988
	127	Mosque lamp, Brs. 5 Piastre.18mm. 2gr	value
	128	Om Kalsoum Ar 1 Pound 5mm. 15 gr	Value, 1976

Recent bank notes illustrating aspects of ancient Egypt

129	LE 10, Khafre	for other sides, 99 & 100
130	Old LE 10 note, Karnak temple	
131	LE 1, Abu Simbel	for other side see 68
132	50 Piastre note, Rameses II	for other side see 67
133	5 Piastre note, Nefertiti	
134	LE 200, Scribe, Imhotep	for other side see 138

Some recent coins

1998	135	Al Azhar 37mm 17.7 gr	1998 LE5
2008	136	LE 1 coin, Tutankhamun, 8.4 gr.25 mm	se
	137	LE1 coin. Value in english & arabic	see 136
	138	50 Piastre coin.	
	139	25 Piastre coin	

A note to be seen with items 69a to 69e, concerning 'A walk in Islamic Cairo'

| | 140 | LE 200 Kani Bey | see 134 |

Appendices

Non-english expressions on currency items

<u>Hieroglyphics</u>
On the:

Coin of Necanebo		Neb nefer. Good gold
50 piastre note		Ra setup en ra ursa maat Ra selects, Ra strong in truth This is the 'throne name' of Ramesses II
LE1 note		Ramesses meri Amen Ramesses beloved of Amen
LE5 note		A U Q T R R Autocrator (The order of hieroglyphics in a cartouche is sometimes jumbled)
LE200 note		Em HoTeP & other heiroglyphics

<u>Mintmarks</u>

Memphis	The khnum
Alexandria, Greek	ΑΛΕΖ
Alexandria, Roman	ALE
Alexandria, Arabic	ا لا دنكسر هي
Paphos, Greek	Π A
Salamis, Greek	Σ A
Sidon, Greek	Σ I
Cairo, Arabic	ا اقا رهه
Egypt, Arabic.	رصم
England; Heaton	H

Other Arabic expressions
The Kalima

ﺍ ﺍﻟﻪ ﺍﻻ	ﻻ	la ilah illa
There is no god except Allah.	ﺣﺮﻩ ﻭ ﺍﻟﻠﻪﺍ	Allah wahduha
He is alone (& has) no partner.	ﻟﻪ ﺷﺮﻙ ﻻ	La sherik lahu
Mohammed is the messenger	ﺍﻟﻠﻪ ﺳﻮ ﺭ ﻣﺤﻤﺪ	Mohammed Rasul Allah Of Allah
Egyptian Sultanate	ﺍﻟﻤﺼﺮﻩ ﺍ ﺍﻟﺴﻠﻄﻨﻪ	Sultanat es Misriyat
King of Egypt	ﻣﺼﺮﻣﻠﻜﺮ	Malik Misr
Republic of Egypt	ﻣﺼﺮﺟﻤﻬﺮﻩ ﺍ	El Jomhuryat Misr

Numerals
Greek
1 A 2 B 3 Γ 4 Δ 5 E 6 Σ 7 Z 8 H 9 Θ 10 I 20 K 30 Λ
40 M 60 Ξ 70 O 80 Π

Arabic
1 ١ 2 ٢ 3 ٣ 4 ٤ 5 ٥ 6 ٦ 7 ٧ 8 ٨ 9 ٩

Arabic dates
 The majority of Islamic coins have dates in the Hijra era, (A.H., i.e. After Hijra) dating from Mohammed's flight from Mecca in 622 AD. The Hijra lunar year of 354 days (i.e. 12 x 28) (sometimes with another day added) is 3% shorter than the Christian year, i.e. 100 Islamic years equal 97 western years.
 So to convert an AH date, e.g. 1255 subtract 3%, i.e. here 37.4, getting approx 1217, add 622 to get 1839 A.D., which is the accession date of Abd al Mejid.

The Sultan Hassan mosque shown on the LE100 note
The plan

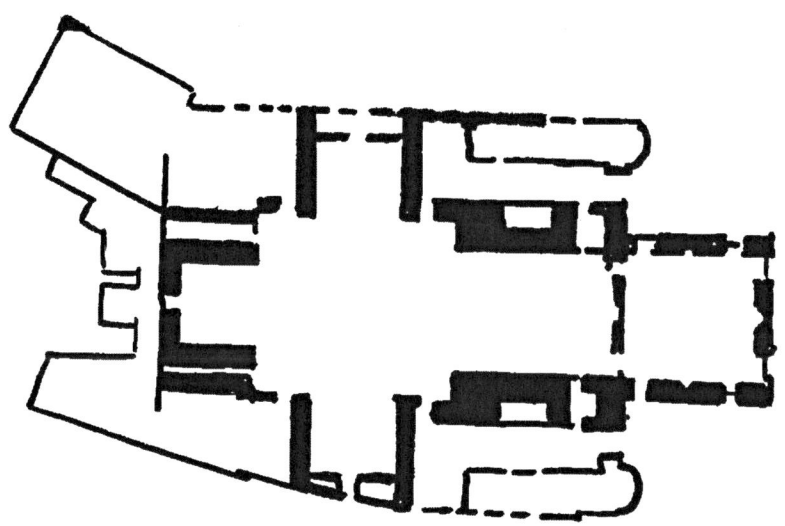

THE DECLINE OF A COIN
THE ALEXANDRIAN TETRADRACHM

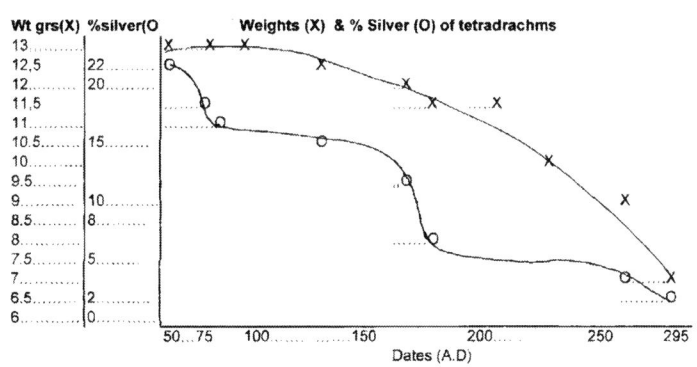

Wt grs(X) %silver(O)   Weights (X) & % Silver (O) of tetradrachms

Wt grs(X)	%silver(O)
13	
12.5	22
12	20
11.5	
11	
10.5	15
10	
9.5	
9	10
8.5	8
8	
7.5	5
7	
6.5	2
6	0

50...75   100...... 150   200....   250   295

Dates (A.D)

C.....N   T............   ..AP......   MA....CO   CII......D

Initials of Emperors

C = Claudi us, N =Ner o T = Trajan,   AP = Antoninus Pius, MA= Marcus Aurelius, CO = Commodus
CII = Claudius 2, D = Diocletian

Bank notes as guideposts for a walk in islamic Cairo.

Medieval Cairo, with its 800 plus monuments, presents a visitor with a daunting problem of how to see these, or even at least a representative selection of them. Many guide books (e.g. Devonshire) divide the city into regions in each of which the important buildings can be surveyed in about a half day walk. Fortunately from our numismatic viewpoint, some current banknotes, noted in the earlier text, provide an ancillary guide to one such walk. If the LE 20 **(98)**, LE 100 **(69d)**, the 2 differing LE 10s **(99) & (100)**, the LE 200 **(140)** and LE 5 **(69a)** notes are laid out in sequence these provide illustrations of major features on a walk from the Citadel to the Ibn Tulun region. A commentary from a guide on this walk might include the following information.

The Citadel was fortified about 1176 by the Ayyubid Saladin as a defence against the Crusaders. Parts of these ayyubid walls are still evident. Within the citadel are three mosques of different periods: there is that of Al Nasir Muhammed (cf **62**), a Mamluk, and that of Suleiman the early Ottoman. These are dominated by the Mohammed Ali mosque, in the late turkish ottoman style, depicted on the LE 20 note. Just below the Citadel, in the Midan Salah ad Din, are the Sultan Hasan and Rifai mosques on the LE 100 and two differing LE 10 notes respectively. The Hasan is actually a madrasa complex. It includes a mosque and the mausoleum of Hasan and around the courtyard are four madrasas or Quranic schools where four aspects of Sunni Islam are taught. (See the plan in this appendix). The complex, one of the finest examples of mamluk architecture, cost 20000 gold coins per day every day for three years to build. This money was obtained, in addition to the usual taxes, from the estates of intestate victims of the Black Death, which struck Cairo in 1348. Next to the Hasan is the Rifai mosque which is a neo-mamluk mosque built in the 1860s. Its exterior and interior are shown on two different versions of the LE 10 note. It is interesting in that it contains the tombs of Farouk and the last Shah of Persia (Iran). By these two mosques, the Hasan and Rifai, there is another mamluk mosque, the Qani Bey built in 1503, and seen on the LE 200 note.

One then has a walk of some 600 metres towards the Ibn Tulun mosque shown on the LE 5 note. On route it is worth noting the Sabil-Kuttab of Kait Bay (1479) A sabil is a public fountain, usually enclosed, providing free drinking water for the public. Often a sabil would have a room above which was for an elementary religious school, the kuttab, for boys. Continuing onwards one comes to the Ibn Tulun mosque, built about 870. Ahmed Ibn Tulun had previously been in Samarra (in Iraq) and the style of his Cairo mosque was influenced by that of Samarra. The Cairo mosque has an attractive simple layout and incorporates pointed arches, some two hundred year before they were used in European buildings. Next to the mosque is the Gayer-Anderson museum. Originally built in 1630, it provides a good example of domestic architecture. It contains an art collection assembled by a British Major after whom the museum is named.

Thus the walk presents examples of abbasid/tulunic, ayyubid, mamluk and both early and late ottoman buildings most of which are illustrated on bank notes.

Bibliography

Selected numismatic bibliography
These titles are in groups corresponding to the sections of the book

Robins G & Shute C 1967	The Rhind Mathematical Papyrus. British Museum London

Ptolemaic

Sear DR. 1979	Greek coins and their Values II. Seaby. London.
Von Reden S. 2007	Money in Ptolemaic Egypt Cambridge University Press. Cambridge
Von Reden S. 2010	Money in classical antiquity Cambridge University Press. Cambridge

Roman

Burnett A. 1987	Coinage in the Roman World. Seaby. London
Duncan Jones R. 1994	Money and Government in the Roman Empire. Cambridge University Press. Cambridge
Lambert R. 1997	Beloved and God. Phoenix. London
Milne JG. 1971	Catalogue of Alexandrian Coins. Oxford University Press. London
De Rouge J & Feuardent F 1979	The Coinage of Nomes of Egypt. Chicago. Obol?
Sear DR. 2000 etc	Roman Coins and their Values. I, II & III. Spink. London
Walker DR 1974	The Metrology of the Roman Silver Coinage. Vol. I & II. B.A.R. London

Byzantine

Bagnall R 2007	Egypt in the Byzantine World, 300 -700. Cambridge University Press. Cambridge

Banaji J 2001	Agrarian change in late antiquity. Oxford University Press. London
Grierson P. 1982	Byzantine coins. Methuen. London.
Johnson AC & West L. 1949	Byzantine Egypt: Economic studies Princeton University Press. Princeton
Sear DR. 1974	Byzantine Coins and their Values. Seaby. (Spink) London

Arabic

Album S 2011	Checklist of Islamic Coins. Album. Santa Rosa
Ashtor E. 1976	A Social and Economic History of the Near East in the Middle Ages. Collins. London.
Bacharach JL. 2006	Islamic History through Coins... the Ikhshidid coinage. American University in Cairo, University Press. Cairo
Balog P 1964	Coinage of the Mamluk Sultans. New York. A.N.S.
Balog P. 1980	The Coinage of the Ayyubids. Royal Numismatic Society. London.
Mitchiner M. 1977	The World of Islam. Hawkins. London
Plant R . 2000	Arabic Coins and how to read them. Spink. London.
Rabie H. 1972	The Financial System of Egypt, 1169-1341. Oxford University Press . London
Valentine WH. 1911	Modern Copper Coins of the Muhammadan States. Spink. London

Ottoman and modern

Pamuk S. 2000	A Monetary History of the Ottoman Empire. Cambridge University press. Cambridge.
Cuhaj GS 2012	Standard Catalog of World Coins. Krause Publications. Iola Wisconsin.
Krause CL & Mishler C 2001	Collecting World Coins. Krause Publications. Iola Wisconsin.
Ditto	Standard Catalog of world coins 1601-1700

Ditto   Standard Catalog of world coins 1701-1800

Sweeny J O 1981   A Numismatic History of the Birmingham Mint Birmingham. The Birmingham Mint

A non-numismatic bibliography

Arrianus F 1958   The Life of Alexander the Great. Folio. London.

Aurelius Marcus   Meditations. Routledge. London.

Copplestone T 1963   (Rawson in) World Architecture. Paul Hamlyn. London.

Devonshire RL 1931   Rambles in Cairo. Schindler. Cairo.

Doxiadis E. 1995   The Mysterious Fayum Portraits. Thames & Hudson. London

Fakhry Ahmed 1974   Bahriyah and Farafra. American University in Cairo Press. Cairo.

Gaddis. 1993   Wonders of Egypt. (Guide booklets) Gaddis. Luxor

Gardiner A 1961   Egypt of the Pharaohs. Oxford University Press. London

Hadas M 1958   A History of Rome. London, Bell

Herodian

Ishaq ibn 1964   The Life of Muhammad. (Ed Edwardes M) Folio

Lane EW (2003)   An account of the manners and customs of the modern Egyptians (1860). American University in Cairo Press. Cairo.

Lane Poole S 1901   A History of Egypt in the Middle Ages. London Methuen

Rawson   see Copplestone

Simpkins. 1992   Splendor of Egypt (Guide booklets) Simpkins, Salt Lake City.

Tacitus   The annals of imperial Rome. Penguin. Harmomdsworth

Vivian C 2000   The western desert of Egypt. American University of Cairo press. Cairo

Wallis Budge   Easy lessons in Egyptian hieroglyphics. Dover,
EA 1910   New York

Wallis Budge   1926. Dwellers on the Nile. London, Religious
EA   Tract Society

Zauzich K 1992   Discovering Egyptian Hieroglyphs. London,
                 Thames & Hudson

Index

Lightning Source UK Ltd.
Milton Keynes UK
UKOW02f1813071114

241306UK00001B/3/P